What People Are S[...]
Threshold Bible Study

"Here, at last, is a Bible study for those of us who don't like Bible studies! Rather than focusing on a book, Stephen Binz invites us to view many well-known passages through the lens of a particular theme, bringing new meaning to the passages and deeper connection to the theme in our own lives. His discussions do far more than inform; they ask for commitment and assent on the part of the reader/prayer."

Kathleen O'Connell Chesto, author of F.I.R.E. and *Why Are the Dandelions Weeds*?

"God's Holy Word addresses the deepest levels of our lives with the assurance of divine grace and wisdom for our individual and communal faith. I am grateful for this new series introducing God's people to the riches of Sacred Scripture. May these guides to understanding the great truths of our Redemption bring us all closer to the Lord of our salvation."

Most Reverend Timothy M. Dolan, Archbishop of Milwaukee

"Threshold Bible Study provides an introduction to some major biblical themes, enabling Catholics to read, with greater understanding, the Bible in the Church. When studied along with the documents of Vatican II and the Catechism of the Catholic Church, this series can be a help for personal and group Bible study."

Francis Cardinal George, O.M.I., Archbishop of Chicago

"Threshold Bible Study offers a marvelous new approach for individuals and groups to study themes in our rich biblical and theological tradition. Moving through these thematic units feels like gazing at panels of stained glass windows, viewing similar images through different lights."

John Endres, S.J., professor of Scripture, Jesuit School of Theology, Berkeley

"Threshold Bible Study offers solid scholarship and spiritual depth. Drawing on the Church's living Tradition and the Jewish roots of the New Testament, Threshold Bible Study can be counted on for lively individual study and prayer, even while it offers spiritual riches to deepen communal conversation and reflection among the people of God. "

Scott Hahn, Professor of biblical theology,
Franciscan University of Steubenville

"The distance many feel between the Word of God and their every-day lives can be overwhelming. It need not be so. Threshold Bible Study is a fine blend of the best of biblical scholarship and a realistic sensitivity to the spiritual journey of the believing Christian. I recommend it highly."

Francis J. Moloney, S.D.B., The Katharine Drexel Professor of Religious Studies,
The Catholic University of America, Washington, D.C.

"Stephen Binz offers an invaluable guide that can make reading the Bible enjoyable (again) and truly nourishing. A real education on how to read the Bible, this series prepares people to discuss Scripture and to share it in community."

Jacques Nieuviarts, Professor of Scripture, Institut Catholique de Toulouse, France

"Threshold Bible Study is a refreshing approach to enable participants to ponder the Scriptures more deeply. The thematic material is clearly presented with a mix of information and spiritual nourishment. The questions are thoughtful and the principles for group discussion are quite helpful. This series provides a practical way for faithful people to get to know the Bible better and to enjoy the fruits of biblical prayer."

Irene Nowell, O.S.B., Mount St. Scholastica, Atchison, Kansas,
Editorial committee for Old Testament translation of the *New American Bible*

"Threshold Bible Study is appropriately named, for its commentary and study questions bring people to the threshold of the text and invite them in. The questions guide but do not dominate. They lead readers to ponder and wrestle with the biblical passages and take them across the threshold toward life with God. Stephen Binz's work stands in the tradition of the biblical renewal movement and brings it back to life. We need more of this in the Church."

Kathleen M. O'Connor, Professor of Old Testament,
Columbia Theological Seminary

"I most strongly recommend Stephen Binz's Threshold Bible Study for adult Bible classes, religious education, and personal spiritual enrichment. The series is exceptional for its scholarly solidity, pastoral practicality, and clarity of presentation. The church owes Binz a great debt of gratitude for his generous and competent labor in the service of the Word of God."

Peter C. Phan, The Ignacio Ellacuria Professor of Catholic Social Thought,
Georgetown University

"Written in a clear and concise style, Threshold Bible Study presents solid contemporary biblical scholarship, offers questions for reflection and/or discussion, and then demonstrates a way to pray from the Scriptures. All these elements work together to offer the reader a wonderful insight into how the sacred texts of our faith can touch our lives in a profound and practical way today. I heartily recommend this series to both individuals and to Bible study groups."

Abbot Gregory J. Polan, O.S.B., Conception Abbey and Seminary College

PEOPLE *of* *the* PASSION

Stephen J. Binz

TWENTY THIRD *23rd*
PUBLICATIONS

All photographs within are the work of the author ©Stephen J. Binz.

The content and format of this study has been adapted from material previously published in *God's Word Today* magazine. The founding editor is George Martin and the present editor is Jean-Pierre Prévost.

The Scripture passages contained herein are from the *New Revised Standard Version of the Bible*, Catholic edition. Copyright © 1989, by the Division of Christian Education of the National Council of Churches in the U.S.A. All rights reserved.

Second printing 2006

Twenty-Third Publications
A Division of Bayard
One Montauk Avenue, Suite 200
New London, CT 06320
(860) 437-3012 or (800) 321-0411
www.twentythirdpublications.com

ISBN-10: 1-58595-314-8
ISBN-13: 978-1-58595-314-1
Library of Congress: 2006922150
Printed in the U.S.A.

Contents

LESSONS 13-18

LESSONS 19-24

LESSONS 25-30

How to Use
Threshold Bible Study

E ach book in the Threshold Bible Study series is designed to lead you through a new doorway of biblical awareness, to accompany you across a new threshold of understanding. The characters, places, and images that you will encounter in each of these topical studies will help you explore new dimensions of your faith and discover deeper insights for your spiritual life.

Threshold Bible Study covers biblical themes in depth in a short amount of time. Unlike more traditional Bible studies that treat a biblical book or series of books, Threshold Bible Study is designed to address specific topics within the entire Bible. The goal is not for you to comprehend everything about each passage, but rather for you to understand what a variety of passages from different books of the Bible reveals about the topic of each study.

Threshold Bible Study offers you an opportunity to explore the entire Bible from the point of view of a variety of different themes. The commentary that follows each biblical passage launches your reflection about that passage and helps you begin to see the significance of the passage in the context of your contemporary experience. The questions following the commentary challenge you to understand the passage more clearly and apply it to your own life. The prayer starter helps you conclude your study by integrating your learning into your relationship with God.

These studies are designed for maximum flexibility. Their format encourages their use both for individual study and group discussion. They are ideal for Bible study groups, small Christian communities, student groups, Sunday school, neighborhood groups, and family reading, as well as for individual learning. Each study is presented in a workbook format, designed for reading, reflecting, writing, discussing, and praying. Space for writing after each question is ideal for personal study and allows group members to prepare in advance for the discussion. The thirty lessons in each study may be used by an individual for daily study over the period of a month, or they may be divided into six lessons per week, providing a group study of six weekly sessions.

The method of Threshold Bible Study is rooted in the classical tradition of "lectio divina," an ancient yet contemporary means for reading the Scriptures reflectively and prayerfully. Reading and interpreting the text (*lectio*) is followed by reflective meditation on its message (*meditatio*). This reading and reflecting flows into prayer from the heart (*oratio* and *contemplatio*).

This ancient method assures us that Bible study is a matter of both the mind and the heart. It is not just an intellectual exercise to learn more and be able to discuss the Bible with others. It is, more importantly, a transforming experience. Reflecting on God's word, guided by the Holy Spirit, illumines the mind with wisdom and stirs the heart with zeal.

Following the personal Bible study, Threshold Bible Study offers a method for extending "lectio divina" into a weekly conversation with a small group. This communal experience will allow participants to enhance their appreciation of the message and build up a spiritual community (*collatio*). The end result will be to increase not only individual faith, but also faithful witness in the context of daily life. Both the individual and group experience will lead participants to actualize the word and live it in the world (*operatio*).

Through the spiritual disciplines of Scripture reading, study, reflection, conversation, and prayer, you will experience God's grace more abundantly and deepen your life in Christ. The risen Jesus said: "Listen! I am standing at the door, knocking; if you hear my voice and open the door, I will come in to you and eat with you, and you with me" (Rev 3:20). Listen to the Word of God, open the door, and cross the threshold to a more abundant dwelling with God!

SUGGESTIONS FOR INDIVIDUAL STUDY

• Make your Bible reading a time of prayer. Ask for God's guidance as you read the Scriptures.

• Try to do your study daily, or as often as possible in the circumstances of your life.

• Read the Bible passage carefully, trying to understand both its meaning and its personal application as you read. Some find it helpful to read the passage aloud.

• Read the passage in another Bible translation. Each version adds to your understanding of the original text.

• Allow the commentary to help you comprehend and apply the scriptural text. The commentary is only a beginning to understanding, not the last word on the meaning of the passage.

• After reflecting on each question, write out your responses. The very act of writing will help you clarify your thoughts, bring you new insights, and amplify your understanding.

• As you reflect on your answers, think about how to actualize God's word and live it in the context of your daily life.

• Conclude each daily lesson by reading the prayer and continuing with your own prayer from the heart.

• Make sure your reflections and prayers are matters of both the mind and the heart. An encounter with God's word is always a transforming experience.

• Choose a word or a phrase from the lesson to carry with you throughout the day as a reminder of your encounter with God's life-changing word.

• Share what you are learning with at least one other person whom you trust for additional insights and affirmation. The ideal way to share learning is in a small group that meets regularly.

SUGGESTIONS FOR GROUP STUDY

• Meet regularly; weekly is ideal. Try to be on time and make attendance a high priority for the sake of the group. The average group meets for about an hour.

• Open each session with a prepared prayer, a song, or a reflection. Find some appropriate way of bringing the group from the workaday world into a sacred time of graced sharing.

• Get acquainted with the other group members, if you have not been together before. Name tags can be helpful as a group begins to meet.

• Spend the first session getting acquainted with one another, reading the Introduction to the study aloud, and discussing the questions.

• Appoint a group facilitator to provide guidance to the discussion. The role of facilitator may rotate among members each week. The facilitator simply keeps the discussion on track; each person shares responsibility for the group. There is no need for the facilitator to be a trained teacher.

• Try to study the six lessons on your own during the week. When you have done your own reflection and written your own answers, you will be better prepared to discuss the six scriptural lessons with the group each week. If you have not had an opportunity to study the passages during the week, meet with the group anyway to share support and insights.

• Participate in the discussion as much as you are able, offering your thoughts, insights, feelings, and decisions. Plan to share what God has taught you during your individual study. You learn by participating and you offer to others the fruits of your study.

• Be careful not to dominate the discussion. It is important that all in the group be offered an equal opportunity to share the results of their work. Try to link what you say to the comments of others so that the group remains on the topic.

• When discussing your own personal thoughts or feelings, try to use "I" language. Be as personal and honest as possible when appropriate and be very cautious about giving advice to others.

• Listen attentively to the other members of the group. Expect that you will learn from the insights of others. The words of the Bible affect each person in a different way, so a group provides a wealth of understanding for each member.

• Don't fear silence. Silence in a group is as important as silence in personal study. It allows time for members to listen to the voice of God's Spirit and gives them an opportunity to form their thoughts before they speak.

• Solicit several responses for each question. The thoughts of different people will build on the answers of others and will lead to deeper insights for all.

• Don't fear controversy. Differences of opinions are a sign of a healthy and honest group. If you cannot resolve an issue, go on, agreeing to disagree. There is probably some truth in each viewpoint.

• Discuss the questions that seem most important for the group. There is no need to cover all the questions in the group session.

• Realize that some questions about the Bible are irresolvable, even by experts. Don't get stuck on some issue for which there are no clear answers.

• Pray as a group in whatever way feels comfortable. Pray for the members of your group throughout the week.

Schedule for group study

Session 1: Introduction   Date _____

Session 2: Lessons 1-6   Date _____

Session 3: Lessons 7-12   Date _____

Session 4: Lessons 13-18   Date _____

Session 5: Lessons 19-24   Date _____

Session 6: Lessons 25-30   Date _____

"If any want to be my followers, let them deny themselves and take up their cross and follow me." Mark 8:34

People of the Passion

S uffering and distress always seem to bring out the best and the worst in our human nature. When crisis comes, some people are overcome with hopelessness, which can lead to despair; others are filled with courage, which can lead to heroism. Still others exhibit a wide range of responses that reveal their character: steadfastness, trust, generosity, weakness, greed, and fear.

One of the challenges posed by the season of Lent is how to be a disciple in the face of hardship and affliction. Jesus stated that the test of true discipleship is related to the cross: "If any want to become my followers, let them deny themselves and take up their cross and follow me" (Mark 8:34). By undertaking the trials of this penitential season, we come to understand the meaning of the cross in our own lives and thus grow in the quality of our discipleship. We become more faithful disciples through caring for the needy, denying our selfish desires, facing our fears, letting go of control, grieving our loses, and forgiving mistakes.

Reflection and discussion

• Why is suffering the best test of discipleship?

• Are times of suffering also the best testing ground for friendship?

• Who do I know who is a model of faithfulness in times of crisis?

The passion accounts of the four gospels are not only about what Jesus did during the final hours of his earthly ministry as he took up the cross; the accounts are about discipleship and the challenges of following Jesus. Through the characters of the passion accounts, each evangelist intended to instruct his readers on discipleship. The people in the passion accounts are examples of the multitude of human responses in the face of suffering and distress. They are examples of the successes and struggles, the challenges and failures, of following Jesus along the way of the cross.

The people of the passion are the characters who participated in some dramatic way in the suffering and death of Jesus. Their stories are told in the four passion accounts of the gospels. Some of them appear in all of the accounts; others only in one gospel. Some of these characters have major roles in the final events of Jesus' life—like Peter and Judas Iscariot; others are mentioned in only one verse—like Simon of Cyrene and the centurion at the cross. Some we remember through their familiar names—like Caiaphas and Pilate. In contrast, some of the most admirable characters remain forever anonymous—like the woman who anointed Jesus and the daughters of Jerusalem.

Throughout each of the four gospels, the portrayal of the chosen disciples of Jesus is remarkably candid. The gospel writers seem to pay special attention to the weaknesses and failures of the disciples. Before the passion accounts, those chosen by Jesus to share in his mission are consistently slow to grasp his teaching; they do not understand his true identity; they protest his teachings about the cross; they are hesitant and fearful in the midst of the storm. But it is in Jerusalem that discipleship is most severely tested. The disciples self-righteously object to the woman who anoints Jesus. One of them goes to barter for Jesus' betrayal. At the Last Supper Jesus predicts treachery by Judas and desertion and denial by the rest of the disciples. During his agony in the garden, his closest disciples cannot stay awake during his most difficult hour. When the enemies of Jesus come for his arrest, his disciples are unprepared and they prove cowardly. One of them responds in direct contradiction to the teachings of Jesus and retaliates with the violence of a sword. All of them abandon Jesus and flee in panic. Peter continues to follow at a distance, but his fears soon overwhelm him as he vehemently denies his discipleship at the moment when Jesus is put on trial. As Jesus is crucified, those whom we would have expected to be near him at the cross have all fled in fear.

It is often the outsiders who seem to exemplify authentic discipleship in the gospels. The sinners and the outcasts are consistently shown to be more open to the message Jesus taught than the righteous. The tax collector, the prostitute, the blind man, the foreign woman, the poor widow: the "minor" characters of the gospels often have more to teach the reader than those with more prominent roles. They may not bear the specific designation of "disciple" or "apostle," they may not have even been graced by Christian tradition with a name, but these unexpected characters in the drama often exemplify genuine discipleship for gospel readers seeking understanding of how best to follow Jesus.

In the passion accounts these unexpected characters come to the fore. The woman at Bethany expresses her love for Jesus in a lavish way by anointing him with expensive oil. Simon of Cyrene carries the cross of Jesus. The women of Jerusalem lament his fate as he makes his way toward Golgotha. The women of Galilee who follow Jesus to Jerusalem remain with him after the male disciples have fled. The criminal condemned to die with Jesus asks for salvation. A Roman centurion recognizes and expresses the true identity of Jesus. Two hidden disciples, Joseph of Arimathea and Nicodemus, come out of the woodwork and give Jesus a proper burial.

Reflection and discussion

• Why would the gospel writers choose the minor characters to demonstrate genuine discipleship?

• What experience in my life helped me sort out my true friends from my fair-weather friends?

Teaching discipleship through the gospel characters

There is no single, clear definition of discipleship in the gospels. Our understanding of what characterizes a true disciple of Jesus must come from the many accounts that depict the relationship Jesus formed with his companions. Following Jesus, staying with him in time of trial, taking up the cross, and remaining at the cross—these are the gospel descriptions of authentic discipleship. It involves following Jesus on a road that leads to his death. Courage, perseverance, generosity, self-sacrifice, devotion—these are the demands that discipleship entails.

The evangelists wrote their gospels for the church of their own day, several decades after the life of Jesus and his disciples. These gospel writers portrayed the characters of the passion in such a way that their readers could relate their own lives to those who were with the historical Jesus. These readers were all faced with the challenge of continuing to follow Jesus in the midst of suffering, trial, and persecution. The fact that the chosen disciples of Jesus all failed in the most critical hour serves as both a warning of what can happen to a committed disciple under pressure and as a consolation that discipleship doesn't have to be perfect. Shaky faith, fair-weather discipleship, apathy and lack of readiness for trial, abandonment, and betrayal of Jesus—Christians in every age reflect the mistakes of the gospel characters.

But the gospels do not leave us in a state of eternal regret and guilt for our failures. Following the passion is the resurrection, which is not only the victory of Jesus over death but his reconciliation of the disciples. The resurrection is the call to begin again. The risen Jesus renews the call of his failed disciples; Jesus forgives them and issues the call again to share in his mission. Those who abandoned Jesus become the nucleus of the new community. The sufferings of the passion have become the birth pangs of new life.

While the chosen disciples have all abandoned Jesus, at his cross stand a disparate group of people: a converted Roman centurion, a member of the Jewish council named Joseph of Arimathea, a group of faithful women who had followed Jesus from Galilee, the mother of Jesus who became the mother of his disciples. Here beneath the cross Jesus has gathered the first preview of what his church will be— women and men, Gentiles and Jews, sinners and saints. The community of the crucified Messiah is open to all—the sinners, the rejected, the poor, the foreigner, the marginal, the converted oppressor, the repentant, all those who search for God. It is not a church of elite and unerring saints, but a flesh and blood Church of frail and failing disciples.

The traditional African-American spiritual asks, "Where you there when they crucified my Lord?" Truly we were all there. In the failures and the heroism of these people of the passion is found the Christian life. This study of the passion is an invitation for us to get inside the heads and hearts of the gospel characters in order to better understand Christian discipleship. Were you there as friend or enemy of Jesus, a genuine or fair-weather disciple, courageous or cowardly, a follower from afar, a cautious onlooker? Through these gospel narratives we are invited to take our own place in the drama because we are indeed people of the passion.

Reflection and discussion

• What are the clearest indications of authentic discipleship today?

• What are the challenges I face this Lent in responding to the call to discipleship?

• What can I do to become a better companion of Jesus?

Prayer

Suffering Lord Jesus, you called your disciples to take up the cross and follow after you. As I study the people involved in the hours of your passion, teach me through their example how to follow you through successes and enthusiasm, as well as through testing and trial. Show me the meaning of the cross. Give me the grace to follow you more completely. Let me share the honor of being named among your disciples.

SUGGESTIONS FOR FACILITATORS, GROUP SESSION 1

1. If the group is meeting for the first time, or if there are newcomers joining the group, it is helpful to provide nametags.

2. Distribute the books to the members of the group.

3. You may want to ask the participants to introduce themselves and tell the group a bit about themselves.

4. Ask one or more of these introductory question:
   - What drew you to join this group?
   - What is your biggest fear in beginning this Bible study?
   - How is beginning this study like a "threshold" for you?

5. You may want to pray this prayer as a group:
Come upon us, Holy Spirit, to enlighten and guide us as we begin this study of the people of the passion. You inspired the writers of the four gospels to write the passion accounts in a way that would communicate God's challenging love for us. Now stir our minds and our hearts to understand these passion accounts as God's good news. Motivate us to read the gospels, give us a love for God's word, and help us to learn the way of discipleship from the people of the passion. Bless us during this session and throughout the coming week with the fire of your love.

6. Read the Introduction aloud, pausing at each question for discussion. Group members may wish to write the insights of the group as each question is discussed. Encourage members of the group to respond to each question.

7. Don't feel compelled to finish the complete Introduction during the session. It is better to allow sufficient time to talk about the questions raised than to rush to the end. Group members may read any remaining sections on their own after the group meeting.

8. Instruct group members to read the first six lessons on their own during the six days before the next group meeting. They should write out their own answers to the questions as preparation for next week's group discussion.

9. Conclude by praying aloud together the prayer at the end of the Introduction.

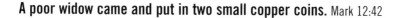
A poor widow came and put in two small copper coins. Mark 12:42

The Poor Widow Gives Her All

MARK 12:38–44 *³⁸As Jesus taught, he said, "Beware of the scribes, who like to walk around in long robes, and to be greeted with respect in the marketplaces, ³⁹and to have the best seats in the synagogues and places of honor at banquets! ⁴⁰They devour widows' houses and for the sake of appearance say long prayers. They will receive the greater condemnation."*

⁴¹He sat down opposite the treasury, and watched the crowd putting money into the treasury. Many rich people put in large sums. ⁴²A poor widow came and put in two small copper coins, which are worth a penny. ⁴³Then he called his disciples and said to them, "Truly I tell you, this poor widow has put in more than all those who are contributing to the treasury. ⁴⁴For all of them have contributed out of their abundance; but she out of her poverty has put in everything she had, all she had to live on."

This account of the poor widow is an overture to the passion account. The woman gives everything that she has, literally, "her whole life" (verse 44). Her offering foreshadows the one that Jesus is about to make—the offering of his very life without reservation.

The scene of the poor widow at the temple is placed next to two contrast-

9

ing images: the greedy, pretentious scribes (verses 38–40), and the rich people putting large sums into the treasury (verse 41). Their actions are marked by self-seeking ambition and outward displays of religious piety. Mark surely intends his readers to see in Jesus' words not only a denunciation of the abuses of Jewish religious leaders but also a warning about the development of similar abuses in Christian circles.

The woman is the one whose action is noted by Jesus because her gift to God is generous and total. When Mark wants to point out a significant event to his readers, Jesus is said to summon his disciples (verse 43). Jesus calls his disciples to take notice of her. She illustrates Jesus' teaching that commitment to God is expressed by wholehearted love rather than the impressiveness of one's sacrificial gift (12:33).

The copper coin was the smallest unit of money in circulation, a minuscule sum. The mention that the woman gave two coins is significant; she could have kept one for herself. The wealthy had probably given what was expected of them, calculated and measured according to the rules for tithing. Yet, this woman's gift is immeasurably greater than theirs because she had given everything. She had let go of every shred of security and had entrusted her whole life to God.

Throughout the gospel Jesus had taught his followers the meaning of discipleship. This woman's deed serves as his final teaching. Discipleship means taking up the cross, laying down one's life, giving one's whole life. The poor widow does not speak a word, yet she is the model disciple. She is one of several minor, often unnamed, characters in Mark's gospel who respond with greater faith than the chosen disciples of Jesus.

Reflection and discussion

• What are the best ways of avoiding hypocritical religious practice?

• What are some ways I can demonstrate the wholehearted devotion of the poor widow in the circumstances of my life?

• In what way is the story of the poor widow an overture to the passion account of Jesus?

• What happens when I let go of the need for security and control in my life and begin to trust God completely?

Prayer

Lord Jesus, you called your disciples to observe the simplicity and generosity of the poor widow. As I study your passion, give me models of discipleship among the people I encounter. May my discipleship be complete, generous, and uncalculating.

**A woman came with an alabaster jar of
very costly ointment of nard.** Mark 14:3

The Woman Who Anointed Jesus

MARK 14:1–9 *¹It was two days before the Passover and the festival of Unleavened Bread. The chief priests and the scribes were looking for a way to arrest Jesus by stealth and kill him; ²for they said, "Not during the festival, or there may be a riot among the people."*

³While he was at Bethany in the house of Simon the leper, as he sat at the table, a woman came with an alabaster jar of very costly ointment of nard, and she broke open the jar and poured the ointment on his head. ⁴But some were there who said to one another in anger, "Why was the ointment wasted in this way? ⁵For this ointment could have been sold for more than three hundred denarii, and the money given to the poor." And they scolded her. ⁶But Jesus said, "Let her alone; why do you trouble her? She has performed a good service for me. ⁷For you always have the poor with you, and you can show kindness to them whenever you wish; but you will not always have me. ⁸She has done what she could; she has anointed my body beforehand for its burial. ⁹Truly I tell you, wherever the good news is proclaimed in the whole world, what she has done will be told in remembrance of her."

The account of the woman at Bethany, like the account of the poor widow, stands out like an oasis in the desert of treachery, greed, and betrayal. Also, like the action of the poor widow, her act of extravagant generosity is a foreshadowing of the unreserved and total love that Jesus will demonstrate in his passion. Notice that the woman did not open the jar and carefully measure out an appropriate amount. Rather, she broke open the jar so that its entire contents were lavishly poured out upon the head of Jesus (verse 3). The aromatic perfume invites us to smell the beautiful scene as we read it with our imaginations.

Nard oil was an expensive ointment that came from the roots of a rare Indian plant. The monetary worth of the oil, calculated at "three hundred denarii" (verse 5), was about a year's wages for an ordinary worker. Those who observed the scene thought that surely this oil could have been put to a more practical use in the form of alms for the poor. The observers understood the value of giving to the needy, but like the wealthy at the temple treasury, they favored a measured and calculated response. The gift of the woman stems from personal love for Jesus. It seems to be an act defying common sense.

Jesus vigorously defended and praised the action of this woman at Bethany as another example of authentic discipleship. Like that of the poor widow, her gift was generous, lavish, and total. The action of this anonymous woman will be told "in memory of her" (verse 9) because she invested her whole self in it. She will be remembered "wherever the good news is proclaimed in the whole world" as a true disciple.

Her loving gesture is interpreted by Jesus as an anointing for his burial. She offers the only anointing of Jesus in the gospel. He is unable to be anointed after this death because of the rapidly approaching Sabbath and unable to be anointed by the women at the tomb because of his resurrection (16:1). Through this anointing the woman gave what she had to Jesus who was giving his life for her.

Reflection and discussion

• What is an example of an action that seems excessive or wasteful, but becomes a beautiful act when done with uncalculating love?

• What have I done recently that has been lavish and extravagant?

• What are the most memorable gifts I have received? What makes them most memorable?

• In what do I invest my whole self? To whom do I give until it hurts?

Prayer

Suffering Messiah, you gave yourself even unto death. Help me learn from those who follow your example of lavish generosity to others. Take away the caution and fears that prevent me from living and giving abundantly.

Jesus came to Simon Peter who said to him,
"Lord, are you going to wash my feet?" John 13:6

Simon Peter Is Taught to Serve

JOHN 13:1–17 ¹*Now before the festival of the Passover, Jesus knew that his hour had come to depart from this world and go to the Father. Having loved his own who were in the world, he loved them to the end.* ²*The devil had already put it into the heart of Judas son of Simon Iscariot to betray him. And during supper* ³*Jesus, knowing that the Father had given all things into his hands, and that he had come from God and was going to God,* ⁴*got up from the table, took off his outer robe, and tied a towel around himself.* ⁵*Then he poured water into a basin and began to wash the disciples' feet and to wipe them with the towel that was tied around him.* ⁶*He came to Simon Peter, who said to him, "Lord, are you going to wash my feet?"* ⁷*Jesus answered, "You do not know now what I am doing, but later you will understand."* ⁸*Peter said to him, "You will never wash my feet." Jesus answered, "Unless I wash you, you have no share with me."* ⁹*Simon Peter said to him, "Lord, not my feet only but also my hands and my head!"* ¹⁰*Jesus said to him, "One who has bathed does not need to wash, except for the feet, but is entirely clean. And you are clean, though not all of you."* ¹¹*For he knew who was to betray him; for this reason he said, "Not all of you are clean."*

¹²*After he had washed their feet, had put on his robe, and had returned to the*

table, he said to them, "Do you know what I have done to you? ¹³*You call me Teacher and Lord—and you are right, for that is what I am.* ¹⁴*So if I, your Lord and Teacher, have washed your feet, you also ought to wash one another's feet.* ¹⁵*For I have set you an example, that you also should do as I have done to you.* ¹⁶*Very truly, I tell you, servants are not greater than their master, nor are messengers greater than the one who sent them.* ¹⁷*If you know these things, you are blessed if you do them."*

Peter learned the first of many lessons he would learn during the passion as Jesus washed his feet. We can imagine Peter's growing apprehension and uneasiness as Jesus took off his outer robe, tied a towel around his waist, and silently washed the feet of each disciple and dried them with the towel. Peter could not contain himself any longer, and when Jesus came to him, he impulsively drew his feet away and told Jesus, "You will never wash my feet" (verse 8).

Jesus told Peter that "now" he does not understand, but "later" he will understand (verse 7). Between the now and later, Jesus will offer his supreme gift of love unto death on the cross. The washing of the feet is a symbolic gesture (like that of the poor widow and the woman at Bethany) expressing limitless and unconditional love. Through this extravagant display, Jesus expresses his love for the disciples, a convincing sign that "he loved them to the end" (verse 1). He loved them to the end of his life and in a way that surpasses all imaginable loving. It is this love that will be expressed in its fullest form on the cross.

When Peter refused the washing, Jesus warned, "Unless I wash you, you have no share with me" (verse 8). Despite his lack of understanding, Peter's task was to surrender himself to the loving gesture and cleansing Jesus was offering, so that he could have a share in the self-giving love that would bring Jesus' life to its end. Then as Jesus had done, so Peter would also do, as he would later follow the "example" of his Lord and Teacher in loving service of others (verses 13–14).

The action of Jesus reverses the customary practice. Footwashing was the task of the servant toward master or the student toward the teacher. The "Teacher and Lord" (verse 13) who washes the feet of his disciples corresponds to the Good Shepherd who lays down his life for his sheep (10:11). Peter, who would be commissioned by the Risen Lord to feed the sheep of Christ's Church, would also lay down his life for them (21:15–19).

Reflection and discussion

• Why did Peter find it so difficult to have his feet washed by Jesus?

• Is it easier for me to give or to receive? Why?

• What can I learn from Peter about surrender?

Prayer

Lord and Teacher, you knelt before your disciples and humbly washed their feet. Impress within my heart this sacrament of your love. Help me to wash and be washed as I give and receive your love.

**Judas Iscariot went to the chief priests and said,
"What will you give me if I betray him to you?"** Matt 26:14–15

Judas Iscariot
Plots Against Jesus

MATTHEW 26:14–25 ¹⁴*Then one of the twelve, who was called Judas Iscariot, went to the chief priests* ¹⁵*and said, "What will you give me if I betray him to you?" They paid him thirty pieces of silver.* ¹⁶*And from that moment he began to look for an opportunity to betray him.*

¹⁷*On the first day of Unleavened Bread the disciples came to Jesus, saying, "Where do you want us to make the preparations for you to eat the Passover?"* ¹⁸*He said, "Go into the city to a certain man, and say to him, 'The Teacher says, My time is near; I will keep the Passover at your house with my disciples.'"* ¹⁹*So the disciples did as Jesus had directed them, and they prepared the Passover meal.*

²⁰*When it was evening, he took his place with the twelve;* ²¹*and while they were eating, he said, "Truly I tell you, one of you will betray me."* ²²*And they became greatly distressed and began to say to him one after another, "Surely not I, Lord?"* ²³*He answered, "The one who has dipped his hand into the bowl with me will betray me.* ²⁴*The Son of Man goes as it is written of him, but woe to that one by whom the Son of Man is betrayed! It would have been better for that one not to have been born."* ²⁵*Judas, who betrayed him, said, "Surely not I, Rabbi?" He replied, "You have said so."*

I n contrast to the outstanding models of generous devotion given in the poor widow and the woman at Bethany, Judas Iscariot expressed the dark side of discipleship. He demonstrated the potential for betrayal possible in every believer in the time of crisis.

The text indicates that greed was one of the motives of Judas for betraying Jesus: "What will you give me if I betray him to you?" (verse 15). Earlier Jesus had warned his listeners, "No one can serve two masters. You cannot serve God and wealth" (6:24). For thirty pieces of silver Judas agreed to hand over his true master to the Jerusalem authorities. The woman lavished her money on a costly gift of perfumed oil for her Master; Judas bargained away his teacher for a paltry handful of silver. With the bargain sealed, the events of the passion have begun their irreversible course.

In response to the prophetic statement of Jesus, "One of you will betray me" (verse 21), each of the disciples ask, "Surely not I, Lord?" (verse 22). All readers of the gospel are pulled into the scene as the question echoes—"one after another"—throughout the room and among disciples down through the ages. The final question comes from Judas, but addressing Jesus with the title "Rabbi" instead of "Lord" (verse 25). The change of title is the evangelist's way of telling us that the problem of Judas is not only his greed but also his lack of true faith in Jesus.

The response of Jesus, "You have said so," is the same response Jesus will give to the high priest (verse 64) and to Pilate (27:11). In each case, the words of Jesus confirm the truth spoken by the questioner. An appropriate translation of Jesus' words might be, "Your own words point to the truth." Jesus lays the responsibility for the decision, the possibility of turning back, and the consequences of the choice squarely upon Judas himself. Judas is not a passive victim of fate.

Reflection and discussion

• What might have been some of the reasons in the mind and heart of Judas for his betrayal of Jesus?

• Is it possible to serve both God and wealth?

• How much does money influence the choices that I make in my life?

• In what situations have I been tempted to betray Jesus for another master?

Prayer

Jesus, I realize my own potential for faithlessness, deceit, and disloyalty. May I continually ask, "Is it I, Lord?" Give me the singlehearted devotion to be faithful to you, my Master and Lord.

One of his disciples—the one whom Jesus loved—
was reclining next to him. John 13:23

The Beloved Disciple Reclines Next to Jesus

JOHN 13:21–30 ²¹*After saying this Jesus was troubled in spirit, and declared, "Very truly, I tell you, one of you will betray me."* ²²*The disciples looked at one another, uncertain of whom he was speaking.* ²³*One of his disciples—the one whom Jesus loved—was reclining next to him;* ²⁴*Simon Peter therefore motioned to him to ask Jesus of whom he was speaking.* ²⁵*So while reclining next to Jesus, he asked him, "Lord, who is it?"* ²⁶*Jesus answered, "It is the one to whom I give this piece of bread when I have dipped it in the dish." So when he had dipped the piece of bread, he gave it to Judas son of Simon Iscariot.* ²⁷*After he received the piece of bread, Satan entered into him. Jesus said to him, "Do quickly what you are going to do."* ²⁸*Now no one at the table knew why he said this to him.* ²⁹*Some thought that, because Judas had the common purse, Jesus was telling him, "Buy what we need for the festival"; or, that he should give something to the poor.* ³⁰*So, after receiving the piece of bread, he immediately went out. And it was night.*

In the context of treachery and betrayal, John's gospel introduces the "beloved disciple" for the first time (verse 23). Though most interpreters from the second century on have assumed that this disciple is John, the disciple remains anonymous in the gospel and interpreters today propose multiple theories of this disciple's identity. The beloved disciple seems to be a historical figure, a person who was greatly influential in the composition of the gospel; but also an ideal figure, the representation of the ideal disciple of Jesus to whom all Christians could aspire.

The close physical proximity of the beloved disciple to Jesus, reclining literally "in the bosom of Jesus" (verse 23) and "on the chest of Jesus" (verse 25), expresses both affection and commitment. John's gospel uses the same expression to describe the intimacy of Jesus with the Father: "close to the Father's heart" (1:18). As the gospel progresses we see that this bond of love with Jesus qualifies the beloved disciple to be a unique witness of Jesus to others, so that they might come also to this level of trust and love.

The scene presents the extremes of discipleship: the failed discipleship of Judas who represents the diabolical powers opposed to Jesus (verse 27), and the model discipleship of the beloved who represents all faithful disciples. Clearly Jesus unconditionally loves them both "to the end" (verse 1). They both experience gestures of his affection: the beloved lying on the breast of Jesus, and Judas receiving a morsel which Jesus dipped in the dish (verse 26), an eastern sign of intimate hospitality. But Judas left Jesus and went out into the darkness to betray him (verse 30); "the disciple whom Jesus loved" will remain with Jesus to the end.

In John's gospel this beloved disciple represents the ideal disciple, the positive qualities of discipleship embodied in one anonymous follower. He is close to Jesus at the Last Supper, standing beneath his cross, and believing in the risen Christ. His faith, love, and dedication are presented in the passion and resurrection accounts as ideal attitudes for all believers.

Reflection and discussion

• Why would the writer of John's gospel leave the beloved disciple anonymous throughout the passion and resurrection accounts?

• Why are gestures of loving affection sometimes more important than words?

• How have times of trial brought out both the best and the worst in me?

• Practically speaking, what does it mean to draw close to the heart of Jesus as Jesus was close to the Father's heart?

Prayer

Jesus, draw me close to your breast so that I can feel the beating of your sacred heart. Draw me into that intimate love which you share with the Father so that I too can be called your beloved disciple.

Peter said to Jesus, "Even though I must die with you, I will not deny you."
Matt 26:35

Peter Vows Fidelity
to Jesus

MATTHEW 26:30–35 *30 When they had sung the hymn, they went out to the Mount of Olives. 31 Then Jesus said to them, "You will all become deserters because of me this night; for it is written, 'I will strike the shepherd, and the sheep of the flock will be scattered.' 32 But after I am raised up, I will go ahead of you to Galilee." 33 Peter said to him, "Though all become deserters because of you, I will never desert you." 34 Jesus said to him, "Truly I tell you, this very night, before the cock crows, you will deny me three times." 35 Peter said to him, "Even though I must die with you, I will not deny you." And so said all the disciples.*

Jesus and his disciples sang the Hallel (Psalm 114—118), the psalms traditionally sung at the end of the Passover meal, which acclaim God's faithfulness to Israel in times of trial (verse 30). In stunning contrast to these songs of trust, Jesus starkly announces that all his disciples will become deserters that very night (verse 31). Despite the nature of discipleship—to be with Jesus—they will all abandon Jesus at the prospect of the cross. They are like the seed that fell on rocky ground. Their discipleship does not have deep

roots and they persevere only for a while. "When trouble or persecution aris-
es" they immediately fall away (13:21). They are like the sheep who scatter
when the shepherd is struck down (verse 31; Zech 13:7).

But seldom in the gospel are predictions of failure or death left unrelieved.
Words of hope are juxtaposed with vignettes of failure. Here Jesus follows his
prediction of the disciples' failure with a prediction of renewal (verse 32).
After his resurrection the wounds of failure would be healed and the disciples
would be renewed in their mission. Once again the shepherd would take his
place at the head of the flock and lead his sheep into Galilee.

One of Peter's endearing and dangerous qualities is his brash confidence.
He is confident that if all the others fail, he certainly will not. His words, "I
will never desert you" (verse 33), directly contradict Jesus' own prediction.
Peter's insistence recalls his earlier words when Jesus predicted his own suffering and death: "This must never happen to you" (16:22). Peter refused to
consider the possibility of failure, and thus he rejects the cross. But Jesus
allowed Peter to fail. In fact, Jesus predicted Peter's threefold denial that very
night, "before the cock crows" (verse 34). Peter affirmed his undying loyalty
to Jesus and set himself up to fall.

Matthew wrote his gospel for the early Christians under persecution. A glorious faith in Christ's divinity easily leads to disillusionment when surrounded by
shame and disgrace. Where is God in the midst of tragedy? The question rever-
berates through human history from the cross into the twenty-first century.

Reflection and discussion

• How am I like the seed that fell on rocky soil (Matt 13:21)? Why is the para-
ble of the sower best tested during times of crisis?

• What is the difference between trust and brash overconfidence? What can I learn from the response of Peter?

• Where is God in the tragedies of our century? Where was God at the cross?

• Why did Jesus allow Peter to fail? Why does God allow me to fail?

Prayer

Jesus, you love me not because I am worthy, loyal, or boldly confident, but because I am dependent on you. Help me accept the reality of my own weakness and to trust in you. Lift me up in times of discouragement and give me faith when I am disillusioned.

SUGGESTIONS FOR FACILITATORS, GROUP SESSION 2

1. If there are newcomers who were not present for the first group session, introduce them now.

2. You may want to pray this prayer as a group:
Lord Jesus, the images of this week's passion accounts are vivid reminders of love and betrayal: the two copper coins, the thirty pieces of silver, the jar of perfume, the towel and the bowl. We want to surround ourselves with reminders of faithful discipleship as we seek to follow in your way. May this gathering of disciples encourage us to listen to God's word, allow it to penetrate our hearts, and put it into practice in our daily lives. Bless us with your Holy Spirit as we learn together the way of discipleship.

3. Ask one or more of the following questions:
   • What was your biggest challenge in Bible study over this past week?
   • What did you learn about yourself from your Bible study this week?
   • What did you learn about discipleship this week?

4. Discuss lessons 1 through 6 together. Assuming that group members have read the Scripture and commentary during the week, there is no need to read it aloud. As you review each lesson, you might want to briefly summarize the Scripture passage of each lesson and ask the group what stands out most clearly about the character in the reading.

5. Choose one or more of the questions for reflection and discussion from each lesson to talk over as a group. You may want to ask group members which question was most challenging or helpful as you review each lesson.

6. Keep the discussion moving, but don't rush the discussion in order to complete more questions. Allow time for the questions that provoke the most discussion. Remember that there are no definitive answers for these discussion questions. The insights of group members will add to the understanding of all. None of these questions require an expert.

7. Instruct group members to complete lessons 7 through 12 on their own during the six days before the next group meeting. They should write out their own answers to the questions as preparation for next week's session.

8. Conclude by praying aloud together the prayer at the end of lesson 6, or any other prayer you choose.

Peter said to Jesus, "Lord, why can I not follow you now?" John 13:37

Peter Offers to Lay Down His Life

JOHN 13:31–38 *³¹When Judas had gone out, Jesus said, "Now the Son of Man has been glorified, and God has been glorified in him. ³²If God has been glorified in him, God will also glorify him in himself and will glorify him at once. ³³Little children, I am with you only a little longer. You will look for me; and as I said to the Jews so now I say to you, 'Where I am going, you cannot come.' ³⁴I give you a new commandment, that you love one another. Just as I have loved you, you also should love one another. ³⁵By this everyone will know that you are my disciples, if you have love for one another."*

³⁶Simon Peter said to him, "Lord, where are you going?" Jesus answered, "Where I am going, you cannot follow me now; but you will follow afterward." ³⁷Peter said to him, "Lord, why can I not follow you now? I will lay down my life for you." ³⁸Jesus answered, "Will you lay down your life for me? Very truly, I tell you, before the cock crows, you will have denied me three times."

Peter's heart is in the right place, but he is continually swept away by his lack of understanding and his misguided enthusiasm. Peter states his desire to follow Jesus and even to lay down his life for Jesus (verse 37). Indeed these are the desires of a good disciple; this is the kind of devotion that Jesus had asked of his disciples. A disciple is one who follows the example of what Jesus has done for his own: "You also should do as I have done to you" (13:15). The way of discipleship is summarized in the new commandment: "Just as I have loved you, you also should love one another" (verses 34–35).

Peter's questions and statements indicate that there is no journey he is not prepared to make with Jesus (verses 36–37). Peter is thinking of a human journey to some adventurous place; Jesus is speaking of his return to the Father. When Jesus washed Peter's feet, Jesus had spoken of Peter's lack of understanding "now" and his understanding "later" (13:7). This same tension is present as Jesus tells Peter, "Where I am going, you cannot follow me now; but you will follow afterward" (verse 36). Between the limitations of the present and the more boundless future is the death and resurrection of Jesus (12:16). The time between is marked by the disciples' ignorance, failure, denial, and betrayal.

Peter's reckless confidence becomes obvious in the contrast between his stated willingness to lay down his life for Jesus and the reality of his actions— the threefold denial before the cock crows (verse 38). But after Jesus is raised, Peter will three times affirm his love for Jesus (21:15–17) and he will prove that love by truly laying down his life for Jesus (21:18–19). Jesus' statement, "You cannot follow me now, but you will follow afterward" (verse 36), refers ultimately to the way that Peter will follow Jesus in leading the early Church and in giving himself even unto death.

Reflection and discussion

• Why do the words of Peter not match his actions? How can I speak with integrity and act with conviction?

• How does the new commandment of Jesus, "Love one another as I have loved you," clarify the meaning of true love?

• What positive and negative qualities of Peter remind me of myself?

• What can I learn from Peter's mistakes?

Prayer

Lord Jesus, in the time before my own return to the Father you have entrusted me with the mission of discipleship. Help me to do to others as you have done, and to love as you have loved.

Jesus took with him **Peter and James and John,**
and began to be distressed and agitated. MARK 14:33

Peter, James, and John Accompany Jesus to Gethsemane

MARK 14:32–42 ³²*They went to a place called Gethsemane; and he said to his disciples, "Sit here while I pray." ³³He took with him Peter and James and John, and began to be distressed and agitated. ³⁴And said to them, "I am deeply grieved, even to death; remain here, and keep awake." ³⁵And going a little farther, he threw himself on the ground and prayed that, if it were possible, the hour might pass from him. ³⁶He said, "Abba, Father, for you all things are possible; remove this cup from me; yet, not what I want, but what you want." ³⁷He came and found them sleeping; and he said to Peter, "Simon, are you asleep? Could you not keep awake one hour? ³⁸Keep awake and pray that you may not come into the time of trial; the spirit indeed is willing, but the flesh is weak." ³⁹And again he went away and prayed, saying the same words. ⁴⁰And once more he came and found them sleeping, for their eyes were very heavy; and they did not know what to say to him. ⁴¹He came a third time and said to them, "Are you still sleeping and taking your rest? Enough! The hour has come; the Son of Man is betrayed into the hands of sinners. ⁴²Get up, let us be going. See, my betrayer is at hand."*

Peter, James, and John were the disciples Jesus led up the high mountain to witness his transfiguration (9:2). Jesus took these same three disciples with him into the grove of olive trees to pray before his arrest. The disciples who were privileged to see his divine glory on the mountain also witnessed his human agony in the garden. Both experiences are necessary for a full understanding of Jesus.

Fully human, Jesus prays with great distress and anguish, prostrate on the ground, asking that his cup of suffering be removed. Luke adds that "his sweat became like great drops of blood falling on the ground" (22:44). Clearly Jesus did not want to suffer and die, though he could have easily escaped by continuing up the Mount of Olives and into the Judean desert. He knows the inner struggle of the will, yet he prays that God's will be done. His prayer echoes the traditional language of the psalms of lament—fear and trembling before death, tormented by the betrayal of friends, surrounded by deceitful and oppressive foes, yet ultimately trusting in God.

The ardent prayer of Jesus is a strong contrast to the drowsiness of his three leading disciples. Before beginning his prayer Jesus had warned his disciples to "keep awake" (verse 34). Jesus urges them again to "keep awake and pray that you may not come into the time of trial" (verse 38). But three times Jesus returns from prayer to find them asleep.

Disciples have to be watchful and alert if they are to continue the mission of Jesus despite opposition and persecution. The willing spirit and the weak flesh (verse 38) will play out their battle in the lives of all disciples. The willing prayer of Jesus to his Father soothed his anguish and strengthened his resolve. But the disciples who failed to watch in vigilant prayer would soon flee in fear. The warning to "keep awake" is a summons to all disciples not to forget, but to be alert and present to the agony of Christ, in whatever person or situation, in whatever time and place.

Reflection and discussion

• Why are the mount of transfiguration and the garden of Gethsemane both necessary for a full understanding of Jesus?

• What were some of the thoughts and feelings Jesus might have experienced at Gethsemane while Peter, James, and John slept?

• Over what issues and realities does Jesus agonize today while I am sluggish and drowsy?

• How can I better respond to the words of Jesus, "Keep awake and pray?"

Prayer

Faithful Son of God, teach me to be alert and pray as you prayed. Help me to pray with hopeful expectation and confident trust, expressing my heart and surrendering myself to the Father's will.

"Judas, is it with a kiss that you are betraying the Son of Man?" Luke 22:48

Judas Betrays Jesus with a Kiss

MATTHEW 26:47–50 [47]*While Jesus was still speaking, Judas, one of the twelve, arrived; with him was a large crowd with swords and clubs, from the chief priests and the elders of the people.* [48]*Now the betrayer had given them a sign, saying, "The one I will kiss is the man; arrest him."* [49]*At once he came up to Jesus and said, "Greetings, Rabbi!" and kissed him.* [50]*Jesus said to him, "Friend, do what you are here to do." Then they came and laid hands on Jesus and arrested him.*

LUKE 22:47–48 [47]*While he was still speaking, suddenly a crowd came, and the one called Judas, one of the twelve, was leading them. He approached Jesus to kiss him;* [48]*but Jesus said to him, "Judas, is it with a kiss that you are betraying the Son of Man?"*

The Mount of Olives was not totally quiet and secluded on the night of Jesus' arrest. The moon was full and crowds of pilgrims were camping out along the slopes of the mount. Political demonstrations and uprisings sometimes occurred during the pilgrimage feasts. Into this crowded scene comes a mob, "a large crowd with swords and clubs, from the chief priests and the elders of the people" (Matt 26:47). They represented the Sanhedrin, the religious ruling body in Jerusalem. The note that the crowd was armed with swords and clubs fills the scene with pending violence. In the midst of this crowd was Judas Iscariot. Luke's account says that Judas was leading the crowd (Luke 22:47).

The arrest of Jesus is a critical moment in the passion account. This "handing over" of Jesus was emphasized in the passion predictions (Matt 20:18) as an element of Jesus' sufferings, along with the trial of Jesus and the crucifixion itself. The tragedy of this betrayal is underscored by noting that Judas was "one of the twelve," one of Jesus' chosen inner circle.

Jesus addressed Judas with the word "friend" (Matt 26:50), highlighting the relationship of trust that had existed between Jesus and Judas. Even more horrible is the sign of betrayal—the kiss. To prevent unrest and uprising among the crowds, Judas and the religious officials had to have a prearranged signal in order to quickly and smoothly seize the right person (Matt 26:48). The kiss—this gesture of loving respect between master and disciple—is distorted by Judas into a signal for arrest. In Luke's account Judas is not given the dignity of speech. As he is about to give the signal, Jesus confronts Judas with the tragic truth: "Is it with a kiss that you are betraying the Son of Man?" (Luke 22:48).

The motive for Judas' betrayal of Jesus has been discussed for centuries. It is possible that Judas handed Jesus over out of greed, for the thirty silver pieces. If so, it was history's most dreadful bargain and the most horrible example of the depths to which love of money can reach. Another possible motive suggests that Judas handed Jesus over in order to compel him to act. Judas saw Jesus as the messianic deliverer who would lead the great rebellion and set up the kingdom. If Jesus were arrested he would be forced to use his powers against his opponents and to begin the great rebellion which, in the mind of Judas, was proceeding far too slowly.

Whatever the motive of Judas, the betrayal with a kiss was an appalling deed. Either motive was compelled by extreme selfishness. Judas refused to accept Jesus as he was and tried to make him what he wanted him to be. Any one of us may think that there must be a better way for Jesus; a better way than the way of the cross. The tragedy of Judas is that he thought he knew better than God.

Reflection and discussion

• Why did Judas hand over Jesus? Why does anyone betray another?

• What meaning does a kiss have for me? How does the kiss of Judas add to the tragedy of the scene?

• Have I ever been betrayed? How does the experience of betrayal feel?

Prayer

Master, you were betrayed with a kiss by one of your own. In the most difficult times—in the darkness, in the midst of the crowd, in moments of confusion—help me to remain faithful to you. Help me to trust in your way and not in my immediate desires.

Simon Peter, who had a sword, drew it, struck the high priest's slave, and cut off his right ear. John 18:10

Simon Peter Fights Back with a Sword

JOHN 18:10–11 ¹⁰ *Then Simon Peter, who had a sword, drew it, struck the high priest's slave, and cut off his right ear. The slave's name was Malchus.* ¹¹ *Jesus said to Peter, "Put your sword back into its sheath. Am I not to drink the cup that the Father has given me?"*

MATTHEW 26:51–56 ⁵¹ *Suddenly, one of those with Jesus put his hand on his sword, drew it, and struck the slave of the high priest, cutting off his ear.* ⁵² *Then Jesus said to him, "Put your sword back into its place; for all who take the sword will perish by the sword.* ⁵³ *Do you think that I cannot appeal to my Father, and he will at once send me more than twelve legions of angels?* ⁵⁴ *But how then would the scriptures be fulfilled, which say it must happen in this way?"* ⁵⁵ *At that hour Jesus said to the crowds, "Have you come out with swords and clubs to arrest me as though I were a bandit? Day after day I sat in the temple teaching, and you did not arrest me.* ⁵⁶ *But all this has taken place, so that the scriptures of the prophets may be fulfilled." Then all the disciples deserted him and fled.*

The other disciples had remained passive during the scene of arrest, but Peter again shows his reckless confidence and draws his sword. He cut off the right ear of Malchus, the slave of the high priest. This violent incident in found in all four of the gospels, but only John's gospel identifies Peter as the one who uses the sword and gives the name of the victim.

Though this scene is interpreted by each evangelist in slightly different ways, they all agree that Jesus condemns the act of violence. He refuses to endorse the use of violence on his own behalf. In Matthew's account, the scene is followed by Jesus' reaffirmation of his teaching on nonviolence given in the Sermon on the Mount (Matt 5:39, 44). Jesus rejects violence as self-destructive: "All who take the sword will perish by the sword" (Matt 26:52). Violence settles nothing; one drawn sword can produce only another drawn sword to meet it. In Luke's account, Jesus shows his compassion in the moment of arrest as he orders his disciples to stop their violence and he heals the servant wounded by the sword (Luke 22:51). By stopping the violence at its beginning, Jesus breaks the chain of retribution which violence provokes.

John's account sets up a strong contrast between the power of the crowd who comes with weapons of violence and the saving power of Jesus. In his trial before Pilate, Jesus states that if his kingdom were from this world, his followers would be fighting to keep him from being handed over. But the source of Jesus' power is not in armed revolution: "My kingdom is not from this world" (John 18:36). Jesus states that he must "drink the cup" (John 18:11); only this act of love, and not the use of violence, can manifest God's redeeming love.

Reflection and discussion

• In what ways is Peter's action typical of his character?

• What is the source of my power? How do I express my power?

• Why is violence self-destructive for those who use it?

• How can I put into practice the nonviolent teachings of Jesus?

• How should I fight for what I believe?

Prayer

Lord of life and love, you taught that violence begets violence and you condemned the practice of retribution. Make me an instrument of your kingdom and a channel of your peace. Help me be brave and courageous enough to fight evil with love.

**A certain young man was following Jesus,
wearing nothing but a linen cloth.** Mark 14:51

The Young Man
Who Ran Off Naked

MARK 14:48–52 *⁴⁸Then Jesus said to them, "Have you come out with swords and clubs to arrest me as though I were a bandit? ⁴⁹Day after day I was with you in the temple teaching, and you did not arrest me. But let the scriptures be fulfilled." ⁵⁰All of them deserted him and fled.*

⁵¹A certain young man was following him, wearing nothing but a linen cloth. They caught hold of him, ⁵²but he left the linen cloth and ran off naked.

At the beginning of the gospel, Mark reports that when Jesus called his disciples, "they left their nets and followed him" (1:18). It was a time of fervent optimism and strong commitment. Here in the most desperate moment of Jesus at the end of his life, Mark reports, "they all left him and fled" (verse 50). The ones who abandoned their nets and followed now abandon their Lord and flee. It is one of the starkest scenes in the Scriptures.

The brief sketch of the young man who fled naked is found only in Mark's gospel. Given the mysterious nature and brevity of the account, the anonymous young man has been the subject of much speculation. As the disciples fled into the night, the crowd tried to seize this young follower. Clothed only in a linen cloth, the man slipped out of his garment and fled away naked. The incident seems to fit the confusion and chaos of the moment.

Earlier Peter had described discipleship in a way that was praised by Jesus: "We have left everything and followed you" (10:28). The disciples have now left everything to flee from Jesus: their commitment, their integrity, their devotion. This young disciple literally left everything, even his clothing, to flee. The fine and costly linen of the cloth left behind emphasizes his fear and desperation. Abandoned by all, Jesus is left to face his arrest and suffering alone.

It was clearly not important for the writer to give a name to this anonymous disciple. Some have speculated that, since the brief verses about the young man appear only in Mark's gospel, he is Mark himself. It is Mark's way of stating that many years before he was an insignificant witness to the final hours of Jesus, listening and watching in the shadows. Perhaps, like the beloved disciple of John's gospel, the young man represents all future disciples. Perhaps he is we.

The disciples followed Jesus until they realized that he was walking the way of the cross. The anonymous young man invites each of us to enter the moment of crisis with Jesus. Will we follow or flee?

Reflection and discussion

• What purpose does the anonymous young man play in the gospel?

• What have I left behind in order to follow Jesus?

• What were the disciples thinking in the moment of crisis? What might I have done had I been there?

• In what way might the young man be me?

• How can I prepare myself now to be faithful to Christ when crises arise in the future?

Prayer

Suffering Lord, you were abandoned by your disciples in your greatest moment of need. Give me strength in time of crisis so that I will hold fast to you in difficult times. You never abandon me. Keep me faithful to you.

First they took Jesus to Annas, who was father-in-law of Caiaphas, the high priest that year. John 18:13

Annas Interrogates Jesus

JOHN 18:12–14, 19–24 [12] *So the soldiers, their officer, and the Jewish police arrested Jesus and bound him.* [13] *First they took him to Annas, who was the father-in-law of Caiaphas, the high priest that year.* [14] *Caiaphas was the one who had advised the Jews that it was better to have one person die for the people.*

[19] *Then the high priest questioned Jesus about his disciples and about his teaching.* [20] *Jesus answered, "I have spoken openly to the world; I have always taught in synagogues and in the temple, where all the Jews come together. I have said nothing in secret.* [21] *Why do you ask me? Ask those who heard what I said to them; they know what I said."* [22] *When he had said this, one of the police standing nearby struck Jesus on the face, saying, "Is that how you answer the high priest?"* [23] *Jesus answered, "If I have spoken wrongly, testify to the wrong. But if I have spoken rightly, why do you strike me?"* [24] *Then Annas sent him bound to Caiaphas the high priest.*

The interrogation of Jesus by Annas is reported only in John's gospel. Annas was high priest of Jerusalem from AD 6 to 15, when he was deposed by the Romans. Yet he continued to have a powerful influence in the religious affairs of the city. Five of his sons reigned as high priests after him, as well as his son-in-law, Caiaphas, the high priest at the time of

Jesus' arrest. Because of his religious influence, Annas continued to be addressed as high priest, though that office was formally held by Caiaphas.

The teachings and actions of Jesus, especially his clearing the temple of those who sold sacrificial animals, threatened the influence and wealth of Annas and his family. As the power behind the throne, Annas wanted to be the first to interrogate this disturbing Galilean. Jesus was a threat to his self-interest and had no hope of receiving justice from Annas.

In John's gospel it is clear that the inquiries before the Jewish high priests were not legal trials with formal charges and witnesses. Rather they were preliminary hearings designed to gather evidence against Jesus so that he could be put on trial before the Roman authorities. The formal trial would be held before the Roman governor, Pilate.

In the other gospels Jesus remains almost completely silent in the face of his opponents. Yet in John's scenes, Jesus challenges his accusers and speaks with open courage as he had throughout his public life (verse 20). When questioned about his teachings and about his disciples, Jesus challenged Annas to learn from those who heard him what he had said throughout his life (verse 21). As a result of the truth-bearing ministry of Jesus, his teachings could now be found among his disciples. Jesus was not a subversive teacher; Jesus had given no secret instructions to a select group. Annas could question anyone who had heard Jesus on any number of occasions and draw his own conclusions.

Annas is reduced to silence before Jesus; Jesus becomes the accuser and Annas the accused. In frustration Annas sent Jesus to Caiaphas, presumably for further questioning. It was Caiaphas who had unwittingly prophesied that "Jesus was about to die for the nation" and "to gather the dispersed children of God" (11:51–52).

Reflection and discussion

• Why was Jesus such a threat to Annas and his family?

• What impresses me most about Jesus during his interrogation by Annas?

• What do I do when confronted with someone whose mind is so made up that the truth doesn't matter?

• How resistant am I when confronted with truth I don't want to hear?

Prayer

Jesus, betrayed, arrested, bound, and accused, help me to realize that the abuse of religion can lead to division, hatred, and violence. Let me learn more of your way of truth and compassion.

SUGGESTIONS FOR FACILITATORS, GROUP SESSION 3

1. Welcome group members and ask if there are any announcements anyone would like to make.

2. You may want to pray this prayer as a group:

Lord Jesus, as we gather as your disciples, help us to realize our weakness and our needs. Like the people of the passion who denied, betrayed, and abandoned you, we are capable of turning away from our calling and denying your grace. Strengthen us with your word, call us anew to follow you, and help us encourage one another. Help us to put out of our lives those things which hinder us from being your committed disciples.

3. Ask one or more of the following questions:
   • With which of the people of the passion do you most identify so far?
   • What is the most important lesson you learned through your study this week?

4. Discuss lessons 7 through 12. Choose one or more of the questions for reflection and discussion from each lesson to talk over as a group. You may want to ask group members which question was most challenging or helpful to them as you review each lesson.

5. Keep the discussion moving, but don't rush it in order to complete more questions. Allow time for the questions that provoke the most discussion.

6. After talking about each lesson, instruct group members to complete lessons 13 through 18 on their own during the six days before the next group meeting. They should write out their own answers to the questions as preparation for next week's discussion.

7. Ask the group if anyone is having any particular problems with his or her Bible study during the week. You may want to share advice and encouragement within the group.

8. Conclude by praying aloud together the prayer at the end of one of the lessons discussed. You may add to the prayer based on the sharing that has occurred in the group.

Those who had arrested Jesus took him to Caiaphas, the high priest. Matt 26:57

Caiaphas Charges Jesus with Blasphemy

MATTHEW 26:57–68 *⁵⁷Those who had arrested Jesus took him to Caiaphas the high priest, in whose house the scribes and the elders had gathered. ⁵⁸But Peter was following him at a distance, as far as the courtyard of the high priest; and going inside, he sat with the guards in order to see how this would end. ⁵⁹Now the chief priests and the whole council were looking for false testimony against Jesus so that they might put him to death, ⁶⁰but they found none, though many false witnesses came forward. At last two came forward ⁶¹and said, "This fellow said, 'I am able to destroy the temple of God and to build it in three days.'" ⁶²The high priest stood up and said, "Have you no answer? What is it that they testify against you?" ⁶³But Jesus was silent. Then the high priest said to him, "I put you under oath before the living God, tell us if you are the Messiah, the Son of God." ⁶⁴Jesus said to him, "You have said so. But I tell you, From now on you will see the Son of Man seated at the right hand of Power and coming on the clouds of heaven." ⁶⁵Then the high priest tore his clothes and said, "He has blasphemed! Why do we still need witnesses? You have now heard his blasphemy. ⁶⁶What is your verdict?" They answered, "He deserves death." ⁶⁷Then they spat in his face and struck him; and some slapped him, ⁶⁸saying, "Prophesy to us, you Messiah! Who is it that struck you?"*

Caiaphas was the high priest at the time of Jesus' death. Caiaphas and Jesus had finally collided. At the house of Caiaphas in Jerusalem scribes and elders had gathered. Matthew's gospel is clear about the purpose of this gathering: they were "looking for false testimony against Jesus so that they might put him to death" (verse 59). The implication is that they knew it was impossible to find a valid accusation, so they had to fabricate a charge that would justify a capital sentence.

Two witnesses finally come forward and make an astonishing charge against Jesus. They accuse him of making the claim: "I am able to destroy the temple of God and to build it in three days" (verse 61). The reader understands that the charge against Jesus has an element of truth. Jesus' authority over the temple is an extension of his identity as the Messiah. He had already stated about himself: "I tell you, something greater than the temple is here" (12:6). Jesus had, in fact, predicted the destruction of the temple (24:1–2), but he had not said that he would destroy it himself.

After the presentation of the witnesses, Caiaphas stood up and demanded a response from Jesus. The silence of Jesus pushed the high priest to put Jesus under oath and ask the climactic question: "Tell us if you are the Messiah, the Son of God" (verse 63). Throughout the gospel Matthew has developed these two titles to proclaim the true identity of Jesus, the same titles of faith that Peter had professed of Jesus (16:16). Jesus responded to Caiaphas in the same way he responded to Judas: "You have said so" (verses 25, 64). This affirmation of Jesus set in motion his journey to the cross. Caiaphas tore his garments, a dramatic gesture that reinforces his belief that Jesus has committed the crime of "blasphemy" (verse 65)—a punishment for which the law of Israel requires death.

Reflection and discussion

• Have I ever been falsely accused? What is my response to false accusations?

• Why did Jesus not defend himself against Caiaphas?

• In what ways is Jesus the true temple of God that will be destroyed and rebuilt?

• What can I learn from the contrast between Jesus and Caiaphas in this scene?

Prayer

Messiah and Son of God, help me to bear witness to you in word and deed. Give me the faith to speak about you to those who need you, and to remain true to you in times of trial.

Peter remembered what Jesus had said, "Before the cock crows, you will deny me three times." Matt 26:75

Peter Denies Knowing Jesus

MATTHEW 26:69–75 *⁶⁹Now Peter was sitting outside in the courtyard. A servant girl came to him and said, "You also were with Jesus the Galilean." ⁷⁰But he denied it before all of them, saying, "I do not know what you are talking about." ⁷¹When he went out to the porch, another servant girl saw him, and she said to the bystanders, "This man was with Jesus of Nazareth." ⁷²Again he denied it with an oath, "I do not know the man." ⁷³After a little while the bystanders came up and said to Peter, "Certainly you are also one of them, for your accent betrays you." ⁷⁴Then he began to curse, and he swore an oath, "I do not know the man!" At that moment the cock crowed. ⁷⁵Then Peter remembered what Jesus had said: "Before the cock crows, you will deny me three times." And he went out and wept bitterly.*

The scene of Peter's denial forms a strong contrast to Jesus standing fearless before the high priest. Like Jesus, Peter is confronted by witnesses. The accusation made against him is that he was "with Jesus" (verse 69, 71), a phrase that expresses the bond between Jesus and his disciples. It is Peter's relationship with Jesus, a bond that had been the meaning of Peter's life, that he denied in his moment of trial.

Jesus had urged his followers to give fearless witness to their discipleship and warned them of the costs of denying him: "Everyone who acknowledges me before others, I also will acknowledge before my Father in heaven; but whoever denies me before others, I also will deny before my Father in heaven" (10:32–33). Peter had boasted, "Even though I must die with you, I will not deny you (verse 35). Yet Peter, who has not yet understood the cross, crumpled under the first challenge and failed to give witness to Jesus.

Peter's threefold denial of Jesus mounts in intensity as he is questioned. When first confronted with the allegation of discipleship, Peter evasively claims that he does not know what the servant girl is talking about (verse 70). Then, questioned by another girl, he explicitly denies even knowing Jesus (verse 72). Finally when the bystanders come to him with the accusation, Peter begins to curse and swear, "I do not know the man!" (verse 74). Peter moves from a vague protest of ignorance to a vigorous public denial of his discipleship.

Peter denied Jesus three times, one denial for each failure to stay awake and pray in Gethsemane. Luke's gospel heightens the impact of the scene by mentioning that, at Peter's final denial, Jesus turned and looked straight at Peter (Luke 22:61). Apparently the interrogation before Caiaphas had just concluded and Jesus was being led down from the chambers where he had been condemned and humiliated.

The cockcrow pierces the scene and Peter remembers the prediction of Jesus and his own determined statement of loyalty. Peter wept bitterly (verse 75) with remorse at his terrible failure. The gospels are staggeringly honest about reporting Peter's denial, an incident that could have easily been hushed up. But in the telling of Peter's sin, the gospels are also telling a powerful story of forgiving love and the wonders of reconciliation.

Reflection and discussion

• What thoughts and feelings might Peter have experienced when he heard the cockcrow?

• When has fear prevented me from doing something I should have done?

• For what mistake am I most in need of God's forgiveness? Have I accepted forgiveness?

• What do I do in situations in which it is embarassing or distressing to be identified as a follower of Jesus?

Prayer

Merciful Lord, you have offered me the privilege of being your disciple and walking the way of the cross with you. May I always acknowledge you and never deny you. Give me strength in times of temptation and forgiveness in times of failure.

When Judas, his betrayer, saw that Jesus was condemned,
he repented and brought back the thirty pieces of silver. Matt 27:3

Judas Ends His Life with Remorse

MATTHEW 27:3–10 *³When Judas, his betrayer, saw that Jesus was condemned, he repented and brought back the thirty pieces of silver to the chief priests and the elders. ⁴He said, "I have sinned by betraying innocent blood." But they said, "What is that to us? See to it yourself." ⁵Throwing down the pieces of silver in the temple, he departed; and he went and hanged himself. ⁶But the chief priests, taking the pieces of silver, said, "It is not lawful to put them into the treasury, since they are blood money." ⁷After conferring together, they used them to buy the potter's field as a place to bury foreigners. ⁸For this reason that field has been called the Field of Blood to this day. ⁹Then was fulfilled what had been spoken through the prophet Jeremiah, "And they took the thirty pieces of silver, the price of the one on whom a price had been set, on whom some of the people of Israel had set a price, ¹⁰and they gave them for the potter's field, as the Lord commanded me."*

No one can truly know or judge the heart of Judas after he realized the consequences of his betrayal. Matthew is the only gospel to narrate what happened to Judas after he handed over Jesus. The gospel tells us when Judas saw Jesus condemned to death, he deeply regretted his betrayal. The word Matthew used to express Judas's change was not the standard word for "repentance" (metanoia), an inner change of heart that leads to forgiveness, but a milder word usually translated as "regret." Yet clearly Judas recognized his mistake and felt deep remorse. He returned the silver pieces by casting them into the temple and he admitted his wrong: "I have sinned by betraying innocent blood" (verse 4). His eternal fate is left to the mercy of God.

Matthew contrasts the reactions of Peter and Judas by placing them before and after the scene of Jesus being handed over to Pilate. Through most of Christian history, Peter has been seen as the repentant sinner who was restored by Jesus, and Judas has been viewed as unrepentant and condemned. Yet a more certain contrast between Peter and Judas is that Peter's denial could be reversed, while Judas' act resulted in the death of Jesus. Judas could not turn back the clock and undo what he had done. Responsibility for the shedding of "innocent blood" (verse 4) was a repulsive offense in the tradition of Israel: "Cursed be anyone who takes a bribe to shed innocent blood" (Deut 27:25).

Both Peter and Judas failed in their commitment to discipleship; they both betrayed their master. Yet, the difference between these two men can be seen in Matthew's final words about each of them: about Peter the gospel says, "He went out and wept bitterly" (26:75); about Judas is says, "He went out and hanged himself" (verse 5). Peter chose repentance and Judas chose death. Peter threw himself on the mercy of God, while Judas despaired of the mercy that Jesus had taught him.

Reflection and discussion

• What feelings might Judas have experienced after his betrayal of Jesus?

• What causes one person to despair and another to repent?

• In what ways have I seen people betray Christ today?

• What does the contrast between Judas and Peter teach me about responding to failure?

Prayer

Jesus, I have betrayed you in difficult times. But I cannot turn back the clock or reverse my failure. You alone know my heart; have mercy on me.

They bound Jesus, led him away, and handed him over to Pilate. Mark 15:1

Pilate Questions Jesus and the Crowd

MARK 15:1–15 ¹*As soon as it was morning, the chief priests held a consultation with the elders and scribes and the whole council. They bound Jesus, led him away, and handed him over to Pilate.* ²*Pilate asked him, "Are you the King of the Jews?" He answered him, "You say so."* ³*Then the chief priests accused him of many things.* ⁴*Pilate asked him again, "Have you no answer? See how many charges they bring against you."* ⁵*But Jesus made no further reply, so that Pilate was amazed.*

⁶*Now at the festival he used to release a prisoner for them, anyone for whom they asked.* ⁷*Now a man called Barabbas was in prison with the rebels who had committed murder during the insurrection.* ⁸*So the crowd came and began to ask Pilate to do for them according to his custom.* ⁹*Then he answered them, "Do you want me to release for you the King of the Jews?"* ¹⁰*For he realized that it was out of jealousy that the chief priests had handed him over.* ¹¹*But the chief priests stirred up the crowd to have him release Barabbas for them instead.* ¹²*Pilate spoke to them again, "Then what do you wish me to do with the man you call the King of the Jews?"* ¹³*They shouted back, "Crucify him!"* ¹⁴*Pilate asked them, "Why, what evil has he done?" But they shouted all the more, "Crucify him!"* ¹⁵*So Pilate, wishing to satisfy the crowd, released Barabbas for them; and after flogging Jesus, he handed him over to be crucified.*

Pilate was the fifth Roman governor of Judea, holding this office from AD 26–35. His central role in the death of Jesus was known by the early Christians and preserved in the early creeds: "Jesus suffered under Pontius Pilate." He needs no introduction in the passion accounts.

The question that Pilate puts to Jesus is the same in all four gospels: "Are you the king of the Jews?" Likewise the same is the response of Jesus: "You say so" (verse 2). Pilate wanted to know if Jesus was a revolutionary, a threat to the authority of the empire. Jesus answers ambiguously, not fully claiming the title of king because of its exalted, political connotations, yet not denying the charge because his kingship is fundamental to his identity as Messiah. The response of Jesus indicates that Pilate has the words right but does not understand the full meaning of his own question. The throne for this king will be the cross.

What is a judge to do with an accused criminal who has not pleaded guilty but who does not assert innocence or deny the charges against him when he is questioned? Pilate is stunned with amazement (verse 5).

Pilate acts neither as a noble judge nor a brave leader, but is swayed by the crowd. He does not want the matter to blow up into a riot, especially during the pilgrim festival of Passover. So, again Jesus is "handed over": Judas had handed him over to the chief priests, the priests had handed him over to Pilate, and Pilate handed Jesus over to be crucified (verse 15). The disciples, the Jewish leaders, and the Roman authorities all share in the responsibility for Jesus' death. Even the crowds share responsibility. There are no mere spectators.

Despite his conviction that Jesus was innocent, that he had committed no crime, Pilate is the one who delivered Jesus over to be put to death. Crucifixion was a Roman penalty used against criminals, runaway slaves, and political insurgents. If the Jewish leaders had put Jesus to death it would have been by stoning, the punishment for blasphemy (Lev 24:16). Pilate had Jesus crucified because he wanted "to satisfy the crowd."

Reflection and discussion
• What else do people do "to satisfy the crowd"?

• Why is it impossible to blame the death of Jesus on any one group of people?

• What are the qualities of genuine leadership? What are the differences between Pilate and a true leader?

• How could the crowd that shouted "Hosanna" when Jesus entered Jerusalem also shout "crucify him"?

Prayer

Suffering king, you were handed over to death by crucifixion in order to satisfy the crowds. Help me to hand over my whole self to you, not to satisfy others but to give glory to you. Reign over my life from your glorious cross.

**Pilate went out to them and said,
"What accusation do you bring against this man?"** John 18:29

Pilate Is Put on Trial by Jesus

JOHN 18:28–40 ²⁸*Then they took Jesus from Caiaphas to Pilate's headquarters. It was early in the morning. They themselves did not enter the headquarters, so as to avoid ritual defilement and to be able to eat the Passover.* ²⁹*So Pilate went out to them and said, "What accusation do you bring against this man?"* ³⁰*They answered, "If this man were not a criminal, we would not have handed him over to you."* ³¹*Pilate said to them, "Take him yourselves and judge him according to your law." The Jews replied, "We are not permitted to put anyone to death."* ³²*(This was to fulfill what Jesus had said when he indicated the kind of death he was to die.)*

³³*Then Pilate entered the headquarters again, summoned Jesus, and asked him, "Are you the King of the Jews?"* ³⁴*Jesus answered, "Do you ask this on your own, or did others tell you about me?"* ³⁵*Pilate replied, "I am not a Jew, am I? Your own nation and the chief priests have handed you over to me. What have you done?"* ³⁶*Jesus answered, "My kingdom is not from this world. If my kingdom were from this world, my followers would be fighting to keep me from being handed over to the Jews. But as it is, my kingdom is not from here."* ³⁷*Pilate asked him, "So you are a king?" Jesus answered, "You say that I am a king. For this I was born, and for this I came into the world, to testify to the truth. Everyone who belongs to the truth listens to my voice."* ³⁸*Pilate asked him, "What is truth?"*

After he had said this, he went out to the Jews again and told them, "I find no case against him. ³⁹*But you have a custom that I release someone for you at the Passover. Do you want me to release for you the King of the Jews?"* ⁴⁰*They shouted in reply, "Not this man, but Barabbas!"*

In John's gospel the trial before Pilate is the heart of the passion account. He expands the dialogue of the trial and heightens its drama. The trial is divided into seven scenes; the setting shifts back and forth from outside the praetorium to inside. Pilate moves from the frenzy of the crowds outside to the eloquent defense of Jesus inside. This dramatic technique expresses the struggle that takes place within Pilate himself as he weighs his own conviction of Jesus' innocence against the pressure from outside to condemn him.

The emphasis throughout the trial before Pilate is the kingship of Jesus. Jesus' condemnation under the pretext that he claimed to be the king is the means John uses in the gospel to reveal the true kingship of Jesus. As in the other gospels, in response to Pilate's question, "Are you the king of the Jews?" (verse 33), Jesus responds ambiguously. But unlike the other gospels, Jesus goes on to proclaim the nature of his kingdom. He is indeed a king, but his kingship is of a very different type. His kingdom is not a political reign belonging to this world, but rather a kingdom that comes from above (verse 36).

The mission of Jesus is to reveal the truth. The truth is the revelation of God made known in the person, words, and actions of Jesus (verse 37). The trial is no longer about the guilt or the innocence of Jesus. Rather Pilate is the one on trial. Jesus' statement, "Everyone who belongs to the truth listens to my voice," implies the question, "Are you on the side of truth, Pilate? Are you listening to me?" The primary issue of the trial is whether or not Pilate will respond to the truth. Pilate's question, "What is truth?" (verse 38), indicates that he rejects the truth revealed in Jesus. Nothing is more contrary to the truth than Pilate and the world he represents.

Reflection and discussion

• What kind of king is Jesus? What does it mean to belong to his kingdom?

• How am I like Pilate in preferring not to decide?

• What decisions do I face that are a choice between truth and falsehood? How do I know the truth?

• What happens in a society when justice is denied and truth compromised?

Prayer

King of heaven and earth, your kingdom is one of truth, goodness, and justice. May I live today as a citizen of your kingdom and proclaim your truth in all that I say and do.

Pilate said to them, "Here is the man!" John 19:5

Pilate Hands Jesus Over for Crucifixion

JOHN 19:1–16 ¹ *Then Pilate took Jesus and had him flogged.* ² *And the soldiers wove a crown of thorns and put it on his head, and they dressed him in a purple robe.* ³ *They kept coming up to him, saying, "Hail, King of the Jews!" and striking him on the face.* ⁴ *Pilate went out again and said to them, "Look, I am bringing him out to you to let you know that I find no case against him."* ⁵ *So Jesus came out, wearing the crown of thorns and the purple robe. Pilate said to them, "Here is the man!"* ⁶ *When the chief priests and the police saw him, they shouted, "Crucify him! Crucify him!" Pilate said to them, "Take him yourselves and crucify him; I find no case against him."* ⁷ *The Jews answered him, "We have a law, and according to that law he ought to die because he has claimed to be the Son of God."*

⁸ *Now when Pilate heard this, he was more afraid than ever.* ⁹ *He entered his headquarters again and asked Jesus, "Where are you from?" But Jesus gave him no answer.* ¹⁰ *Pilate therefore said to him, "Do you refuse to speak to me? Do you not know that I have power to release you, and power to crucify you?"* ¹¹ *Jesus answered him, "You would have no power over me unless it had been given you from above; therefore the one who handed me over to you is guilty of a greater sin."* ¹² *From then on Pilate tried to release him, but the Jews cried out, "If you*

release this man, you are no friend of the emperor. Everyone who claims to be a king sets himself against the emperor."

¹³*When Pilate heard these words, he brought Jesus outside and sat on the judge's bench at a place called the Stone Pavement, or in Hebrew Gabbatha.* ¹⁴*Now it was the day of Preparation for the Passover; and it was about noon. He said to the Jews, "Here is your King!"* ¹⁵*They cried out, "Away with him! Away with him! Crucify him!" Pilate asked them, "Shall I crucify your King?" The chief priests answered, "We have no king but the emperor."* ¹⁶*Then he handed him over to them to be crucified.*

In the trial before Pilate, John presents us with a dramatic confrontation between the divine and the human. The questions and motives of Pilate are on the worldly level; the responses of Jesus indicate that he is speaking and acting on a higher level. Pilate tries to avoid having to decide between truth and falsehood. Yet it becomes increasingly clearer that Pilate will not be able to escape making a judgment about the truth, and this leads him to become "more afraid than ever" (verse 8). Truly Pilate is the one on trial before his divine judge.

All the gospels offer the impression that Pilate's condemnation of Jesus was under public coercion and against Pilate's better judgment. He tries to minimize the significance of Jesus by mocking his kingship with the crown of thorns and the purple cloak, and by displaying his miserable condition to the crowds. Pilate's acclamation, "Here is the man!" (verse 5), presents Jesus as an unfortunate and miserable man who should not be taken seriously. Yet the reader of John's gospel knows that this is the suffering Son of Man on the way to glory (12:23).

When Pilate tried to use his authority to release Jesus, the religious leaders played their trump card. "If you release this man you are no friend of the emperor" (verse 12), they shouted. Because anyone who claimed to be king opposes the emperor, by setting Jesus free Pilate would be risking his honorary status as "friend of Caesar" as well as his position as Roman procurator. Continually fearful, Pilate ironically proclaimed the truth about Jesus as he continued to mock his royalty. Presenting Jesus to the crowds, Pilate proclaimed, "Here is your king!" (verse 14). At the site of crucifixion, Pilate has an inscription written and placed upon the cross, "Jesus of Nazareth, the King of the Jews" (19:19).

John's gospel notes that Pilate handed Jesus over to be crucified at about noon on the Day of Preparation for the Passover (verse 14). This is the very hour that the Passover lambs began to be ritually slaughtered in the temple. While thousands of lambs were being killed in preparation for the great feast of liberation, the Lamb of God who takes away the sin of the world (1:29) is offered up on the cross.

Reflection and discussion

• When the pressure from the crowd increased, Pilate became "more afraid than ever" (verse 8). In what ways do my fears paralyze me?

• In what ways does Pilate's mockery of Jesus ironically proclaim the truth about him?

Prayer

Son of Man, you were mocked and condemned by fearful men who refused to acknowledge the truth. May I acknowledge you as the way, the truth, and the life by my words and actions.

SUGGESTIONS FOR FACILITATORS, GROUP SESSION 4

1. Welcome group members and ask if anyone has any questions, announcements, or requests.

2. You may want to pray this prayer as a group:

Lord Jesus, like the people in these passion accounts, each of us come to this group filled with many fears. You alone know our hearts completely. Help us to acknowledge our fears so that we may face them confidently, assured of your grace. Calm our insecurities and our worries; give us confidence with the inspiration of the Scriptures. As your word empowers us to know the truth, give us the courage we need to acknowledge the truth and to make choices that will lead us to you, who are the way, the truth, and the life.

3. Ask one or more of the following questions:
   - What is the most difficult part of this study for you?
   - What did you learn about yourself this week?

4. Discuss lessons 13 through 18. Choose one or more of the questions for reflection and discussion from each lesson to discuss as a group. You may want to ask group members which question was most challenging or helpful to them as you review each lesson.

5. Keep the discussion moving, but allow time for the questions that provoke the most discussion. Encourage the group members to use "I" language in their responses.

6. After talking over each lesson, instruct group members to complete lessons 19 through 24 on their own during the six days before the next group meeting. They should write out their own answers to the questions as preparation for next week's session.

7. Ask the group how this study is affecting the way they experience the days of Lent this year. Discuss challenges and encourage one another during the remaining days of Lent.

8. Conclude by praying aloud together the prayer at the end of one of the lessons discussed. You may choose to conclude the prayer by asking members to pray aloud any requests they may have.

When Herod saw Jesus he was very glad,
for he had been wanting to see him for a long time. Luke 23:8

Herod Mocks Jesus

LUKE 23:6–15 ⁶*When Pilate heard this, he asked whether the man was a Galilean. ⁷And when he learned that he was under Herod's jurisdiction, he sent him off to Herod, who was himself in Jerusalem at that time. ⁸When Herod saw Jesus, he was very glad, for he had been wanting to see him for a long time, because he had heard about him and was hoping to see him perform some sign. ⁹He questioned him at some length, but Jesus gave him no answer. ¹⁰The chief priests and the scribes stood by, vehemently accusing him. ¹¹Even Herod with his soldiers treated him with contempt and mocked him; then he put an elegant robe on him, and sent him back to Pilate. ¹²That same day Herod and Pilate became friends with each other; before this they had been enemies.*

¹³Pilate then called together the chief priests, the leaders, and the people, ¹⁴and said to them, "You brought me this man as one who was perverting the people; and here I have examined him in your presence and have not found this man guilty of any of your charges against him. ¹⁵Neither has Herod, for he sent him back to us. Indeed, he has done nothing to deserve death."

When Pilate learned that Jesus was from Galilee, he diverted the trial to Herod, the ruler of Galilee, who would have jurisdiction over Jesus in his home territory. This Herod, known as Herod

Antipas, had played a significant role throughout the gospel of Luke. He is portrayed as a corrupt and decadent leader who wished to destroy Jesus.

Jesus was born during the reign of Herod's father, Herod the Great (1:5). During the adult life of Jesus, Herod Antipas imprisoned John (3:19–20), and later had John beheaded. Twice Luke's gospel tells us that Herod wanted to see Jesus after hearing about his reputation (verse 8; 9:9). When Jesus was informed that Herod wanted to kill him, Jesus lashed out, calling Herod a "fox" (13:31–32), an animal known to be sly, crafty, and destructive.

Herod was in Jerusalem for the feast of Passover, probably a politically motivated gesture. When Jesus was sent to him, he questioned him at great length (verse 9), treated him with contempt (verse 11), and mockingly clothed him in a regal cloak (verse 11). Herod's desire to see Jesus and "to see him perform some sign" (verse 8) indicates that Herod thought of Jesus simply as a spectacle, an attention-grabbing exhibit, a curiosity to be shown off in his court. He jested at Jesus, ridiculed him, and refused to take him seriously. Like Pilate, Herod judged Jesus not guilty of the accusations before him (verses 14–15), yet they both share responsibility for condemning him to death.

The great irony of this encounter is expressed in the reconciliation of Herod and Pilate who had previously been enemies (verse 12). Though Jesus was humiliated by these two ruthless representatives of worldly power, in his suffering he brought them together in friendship. Through his work of healing and forgiveness, Jesus provided an occasion of grace even for Herod and Pilate.

Reflection and discussion

• Why might Herod have been so eager to see Jesus? What questions might Herod have asked Jesus?

• Herod saw Jesus as a wonder-working spectacle. Do I ever look upon Jesus in this way?

• Why did Herod ridicule Jesus and refuse to take him seriously?

• What is the difference between the kingship of Jesus and the authority of Herod?

• How could the passion of Jesus bring about healing between two enemies?

Prayer

King of the ages, you were mocked and humiliated by ruthless and corrupt people. Yet, in your passion you brought forgiveness and healing to all who would accept it. Have mercy on me and forgive me for the times I refused to take you seriously.

"Whom do you want me to release to you,
Jesus Barabbas or Jesus who is called the Messiah?" Matt 27:17

Barabbas Is Released
While Jesus Is Condemned

MATTHEW 27:15–26 ¹⁵ *Now at the festival the governor was accustomed to release a prisoner for the crowd, anyone whom they wanted.* ¹⁶ *At that time they had a notorious prisoner, called Jesus Barabbas.* ¹⁷ *So after they had gathered, Pilate said to them, "Whom do you want me to release for you, Jesus Barabbas or Jesus who is called the Messiah?"* ¹⁸ *For he realized that it was out of jealousy that they had handed him over.* ¹⁹ *While he was sitting on the judgment seat, his wife sent word to him, "Have nothing to do with that innocent man, for today I have suffered a great deal because of a dream about him."* ²⁰ *Now the chief priests and the elders persuaded the crowds to ask for Barabbas and to have Jesus killed.* ²¹ *The governor again said to them, "Which of the two do you want me to release for you?" And they said, "Barabbas."* ²² *Pilate said to them, "Then what should I do with Jesus who is called the Messiah?" All of them said, "Let him be crucified!"* ²³ *Then he asked, "Why, what evil has he done?" But they shouted all the more, "Let him be crucified!"*

²⁴ *So when Pilate saw that he could do nothing, but rather that a riot was beginning, he took some water and washed his hands before the crowd, saying, "I am innocent of this man's blood; see to it yourselves."* ²⁵ *Then the people as a*

whole answered, "His blood be on us and on our children!" [26]*So he released Barabbas for them; and after flogging Jesus, he handed him over to be crucified.*

The custom of releasing a prisoner at Passover seems to have been a concession to the Jews, a conciliatory gesture on the part of the Roman government. Nationalistic fervor was often at a boiling point during the feast of Israel's liberation, and allowing the Jews to choose a prisoner for release was meant to cool their passions. The populace of Jerusalem seems to be the agent in choosing the one to be released. Matthew's gospel builds up this scene as the climactic choice in the passion narrative.

The name Barabbas literally means "son of the father," providing an ironic choice between Barabbas and the true Son of the Father. Some ancient manuscripts read "Jesus Barabbas" in verse 16 and 17. Since Jesus was a common Jewish name, it is probable that this was the original reading and that later the name Jesus was eliminated from the text out of respect for the name. Matthew calls him a "notorious prisoner" (verse 16); Mark and Luke note that he was "in prison with the rebels who had committed murder during the insurrection" (Mark 15:7; Luke 23:19, 25).

When confronted with Jesus and his message, people must ultimately choose to accept or reject him. The decision is set before the crowd in Pilate's final question: "Which of the two do you want me to release for you" (verse 21). It was the chief priests and elders who persuaded the crowd to choose Barabbas for release and to call for Jesus' death (verse 20). Pilate gave in to the demands of the crowds, despite his wife's warning (verse 19), only when he realized that he had not succeeded in convincing them of Jesus' innocence and that a riot was breaking out as the shouts of the crowds grew louder (verse 24).

The historical choice between Jesus or Barabbas during the passion represents the continual choice that everyone must make. Perhaps Pilate's wife represents the divine voice that we can hear in those we love, urging us to do the right and to act with integrity. Will we choose Jesus, the Father's Son, or will we choose another way?

Reflection and discussion

• In what way does Barabbas represent me in the passion accounts?

• How do I respond to conflicting pressures? How do I make a decision about the big choices in my life?

• In view of her comments in the trial of Jesus, what might the role of Pilate's wife have been throughout her husband's life?

• What might the rest of life been like for Barabbas after being released?

Prayer

Son of the Father, you gave up your life in place of Barabbas and in place of us all. Thank you for releasing me from punishment and guilt, and for giving your life for my eternal freedom.

The soldiers of the governor took Jesus into the governor's headquarters, and they gathered the whole cohort around him. Matt 27:27

The Soldiers Mock and Torture Jesus

MATTHEW 27:27–31 [27] *Then the soldiers of the governor took Jesus into the governor's headquarters, and they gathered the whole cohort around him.* [28] *They stripped him and put a scarlet robe on him,* [29] *and after twisting some thorns into a crown, they put it on his head. They put a reed in his right hand and knelt before him and mocked him, saying, "Hail, King of the Jews!"* [30] *They spat on him, and took the reed and struck him on the head.* [31] *After mocking him, they stripped him of the robe and put his own clothes on him. Then they led him away to crucify him.*

The soldiers who mocked and tortured Jesus were under Roman command and were conscripted from different parts of the empire. They were from one of the several cohorts of soldiers at Pilate's disposal, trained to subjugate oppressed people and detailed for crucifixion duty.

The buffoonery by the soldiers consisted of a charade to a mock king. They dressed Jesus in a scarlet cloak (verse 28). The other gospels speak of a purple cloak, the color most associated with royalty. But scarlet was the customary color of the soldiers' outer tunic. They twisted a thorny spiked crown and put it on his head. "Crowns" at this time were ornamental headbands or wreaths, not the crowns of later royalty, so the crown of thorns would resemble a spiked wreath. The reed placed in Jesus' right hand was intended to imitate a royal scepter (verse 29).

The mock coronation and mock homage acclaimed Jesus with the title used in accusation against him during his trial by Pilate: "Hail, King of the Jews." It was a burlesque of the "Hail Caesar" acclamation of the emperor. The supreme irony of the scene, of course, is that Jesus truly is the king of both Jews and Gentiles and his mockery proclaims the truth of his identity. He is the King of kings, at whose name every knee will bow.

The mockery soon turns from derision to physical abuse. Matthew presents a scene of escalating violence: the soldiers knelt, spat, and struck Jesus. The whips used in Roman floggings were leather thongs, studded at intervals with sharpened bits of bone or pellets of lead that would rip through the victim's skin and muscle tissue. The inflamed and bleeding body often lost so much blood that the victim was unable to carry the cross to the place of execution.

The brutality of the scene is in direct contrast to the nonviolent teachings of Jesus (26:52). He taught his followers not to meet violence with violence and follows his own teaching as he submits to the violence against him. This violence by the soldiers is a cruel prelude to the path to Golgotha.

Reflection and discussion

• Who are the victims of mockery and abuse today?

• What are the pros and cons of highlighting the physical torture of Jesus in movies and other dramatic depictions of the passion?

• What forms of injustice make my blood boil? What can I do about the cruelty and violence in our world?

• How do I decide when to fight for what is right, and when not to?

• Are the nonviolent teachings of Jesus practical and applicable in our society today?

Prayer

Suffering Servant, help me to see your crucified body in the victims of abuse and cruelty today. Give me the courage to defend victims of injustice and to demonstrate your compassion.

They compelled a passer-by to carry his cross;
it was Simon of Cyrene. Mark 15:21

Simon of Cyrene Carries the Cross

MARK 15:21–22 *²¹ They compelled a passer-by, who was coming in from the country, to carry his cross; it was Simon of Cyrene, the father of Alexander and Rufus. ²² Then they brought Jesus to the place called Golgotha (which means the place of a skull).*

ROMANS 16:13 *¹³ Greet Rufus, chosen in the Lord; and greet his mother—a mother to me also.*

Simon of Cyrene was a Jewish man who had arrived from northern Africa, possibly fulfilling a life's ambition to come to Jerusalem for the pilgrim feast of Passover. Cyrene was the capital of the district of Cyrenaica in Lydia where there was a sizable Jewish population.

Unlike later artists depicting the crucifixion, first century readers of the gospel would have understood that only the horizontal crossbeam was carried as Jesus was lead out of Jerusalem. Roman writings indicate that criminals would normally carry the crossbeam through the city before being crucified to it. The vertical beam of the cross stood already implanted at the place of execution. The crossbeam was usually carried behind the nape of the neck like a yoke, with the criminal's arms pulled back and hooked over it.

Simon of Cyrene apparently was a previously unknown passerby who was coming in from the surrounding countryside when the soldiers were leading Jesus out of the city (verse 21). The soldiers coerced Simon into his role of taking up the crossbeam, probably because Jesus was already so physically weak from his torturous flogging. What must have seemed to Simon at first a terrible indignity, carrying the cross of a condemned man, became his moment of glory. On that awful day Jesus laid hold of Simon's heart and changed his life forever.

The words used here, "carry (take up) his cross," are the exact words Jesus used when first teaching his disciples about the way of suffering: "If any want to become my followers, let them deny themselves and take up their cross and follow me" (8:34). The brief verse that recalls the action of Simon carrying the cross is a reminder to all believers of the cost of discipleship. After the chosen disciples of Jesus had fled, Simon of Cyrene represents the true disciple.

The names of Simon and his sons, Alexander and Rufus (Mark 15:21), must have been known to the early church to which Mark's gospel was written. Perhaps they were members of the Christian community in Rome, the most probable original audience for the gospel. Rufus, the one "chosen in the Lord," is affectionately noted along with his mother in Paul's closing words to the Romans (Rom 16:13). Rufus' mother, the wife of Simon, was so dear to Paul that he called her his own spiritual mother. We may speculate that the whole family of Simon became disciples and eventually settled in Rome. One moment with Jesus is enough to change the life of generations forever.

Reflection and discussion

• In what way does Simon represent the true disciple in the passion account?

• What might have happened to change Simon's life forever on that fateful day at Golgotha?

• What is the cross Jesus has called me to carry? How does that cross make me a better disciple?

• How does my cross help others to see Jesus and inspire them to follow him?

Prayer

Jesus, bearer of the cross, you have called me to take up the cross and follow in your way. Teach me to recognize my cross and give me the strength to bear it in love.

"Daughters of Jerusalem, do not weep for me,
but weep for yourselves and for your children." Luke 23:28

The Women of Jerusalem
Weep for Jesus

LUKE 23:27–31 *²⁷A great number of the people followed him, and among them were women who were beating their breasts and wailing for him. ²⁸But Jesus turned to them and said, "Daughters of Jerusalem, do not weep for me, but weep for yourselves and for your children. ²⁹For the days are surely coming when they will say, 'Blessed are the barren, and the wombs that never bore, and the breasts that never nursed.' ³⁰Then they will begin to say to the mountains, 'Fall on us'; and to the hills, 'Cover us.' ³¹For if they do this when the wood is green, what will happen when it is dry?"*

Luke reports that among the crowd of people who followed Jesus along the way of the cross was a group of women from Jerusalem. They were clearly sympathetic toward Jesus in contrast to those who abused and mocked him. The women were "beating their breasts and wailing for him" (verse 27), mourning and lamenting what was happening to Jesus.

Jesus addresses them as "daughters of Jerusalem." This scene is sometimes wrongly entitled, "Jesus consoles the women of Jerusalem." The words of Jesus are clearly not a consolation. He speaks like a prophet of old and pronounces a judgment upon the city. He urges the women not to lament for him but for themselves and their children (verse 28).

Jesus knows that the days are coming when Jerusalem will be brutally besieged by the Romans in AD 70 (see 19:42–44). The destruction and suffering of those days will be so great that people will say: "Blessed are the barren, and the wombs that never bore and the breasts that never nursed" (verse 29). It is a tragic beatitude. Instead of sterility being a curse, as it always was in the Hebrew Bible, it becomes a blessing. It is better not to have children and be spared seeing them suffer and die. The experience will be so dreadful that people will wish for death and burial (verse 30) to put an end to the horrors.

The final statement of Jesus to the women compares his own suffering to "green wood" and the later suffering of Jerusalem as "dry wood" (verse 31). If Jerusalem can put to death its innocent Messiah, who is like "green wood" not meant for the fire, how much more destruction is destined to fall upon this city, which is like dry wood ready for burning. Besides these pessimistic words, the crucifixion scene in Luke's gospel also contains a note of hope for Jerusalem. After the death of Jesus, Luke adds that the crowds "returned home, beating their breasts" (verse 48), a gesture of contrition and repentance.

Reflection and discussion

• Why do the gospel writers portray women in a mostly favorable light in the passion accounts?

• What did Jesus mean in the tragic beatitude of verse 29?

• What are my greatest fears for my children or for the children of others?

• Knowing that suffering will be an inevitable part of their lives, is it worth bringing children into the world?

• What is the meaning of the proverb in verse 31?

Prayer

Lord of Life, through my parents you gave me life. Through children you give me the privilege to nurture your life. Help me to love the children of our world and to give them hope.

Two others, who were criminals, were led away to be put to death with Jesus. Luke 23:32

Two Criminals Travel the Way of Crucifixion with Jesus

LUKE 23:32–43 *³²Two others also, who were criminals, were led away to be put to death with him. ³³When they came to the place that is called The Skull, they crucified Jesus there with the criminals, one on his right and one on his left. ³⁴Then Jesus said, "Father, forgive them; for they do not know what they are doing." And they cast lots to divide his clothing. ³⁵And the people stood by, watching; but the leaders scoffed at him, saying, "He saved others; let him save himself if he is the Messiah of God, his chosen one!" ³⁶The soldiers also mocked him, coming up and offering him sour wine, ³⁷and saying, "If you are the King of the Jews, save yourself!" ³⁸There was also an inscription over him, "This is the King of the Jews."*

³⁹One of the criminals who were hanged there kept deriding him and saying, "Are you not the Messiah? Save yourself and us!" ⁴⁰But the other rebuked him, saying, "Do you not fear God, since you are under the same sentence of condemnation? ⁴¹And we indeed have been condemned justly, for we are getting what we deserve for our deeds, but this man has done nothing wrong." ⁴²Then he said,

"Jesus, remember me when you come into your kingdom." [43] *He replied, "Truly I tell you, today you will be with me in Paradise."*

Luke tells us that two condemned criminals accompanied Jesus on the way to crucifixion (verse 32). Throughout his life Jesus had a particular bond with sinners and outcasts, earning the contempt of his enemies by even eating with them. Now Jesus would walk to his death with these kinds of companions.

These two criminals were crucified with Jesus, "one on his right and one on his left" (verse 33). The words of these two criminals while hanging on their crosses reveal two drastically different responses to Jesus. The unrepentant criminal joins in the mockery, challenging Jesus to save himself if he is the Messiah (verses 35–36, 39). But the words of the other criminal reveal a radically different attitude, a step-by-step process of conversion.

First, the repentant criminal confesses his sins: "We indeed have been condemned justly, for we are getting what we deserve for our deeds" (verse 41). Then he turns to Jesus for help: "Jesus, remember me when you come into your kingdom" (verse 42). The sinner calls on the name of Jesus, recognizing that in his death, Jesus is the source of his salvation.

While the repentant criminal hoped for some future salvation, when Jesus comes into his kingdom, the response of Jesus indicates that salvation is immediate: "Truly I tell you, today you will be with me in Paradise" (verse 43). Jesus, the one who came "to seek out and to save the lost" (19:10), continued to welcome the outcast and the sinner until his final breath. Jesus died as he had lived, extending his saving mercy to all.

There are many things in our lives for which we might truly say, "It is too late. The time for that is past." But we can never say that of turning to Jesus Christ. The one who forgave his executioners, "Father, forgive them" (verse 34), will forgive us at whatever point in our life we turn to him. It is never too late to receive the salvation that Christ offers us.

Reflection and discussion

• What do I want to remember when I see the image of three crosses on Calvary?

• What does the kind of company Jesus kept tell us about his character?

• What does the repentant criminal teach me about the process of repentance?

• What do I think of people who turn to Christ in the final hours of life?

Prayer

Merciful Savior, you prayed that your Father forgive those who put you to death. You have forgiven me time and time again, when I did not deserve your mercy. Help me to live a life of gratitude.

SUGGESTIONS FOR FACILITATORS, GROUP SESSION 5

1. Welcome group members and ask if anyone has any questions, announcements, or requests.

2. You may want to pray this prayer as a group:

Lord Jesus, we come overwhelmed by the violence and cruelty that plagues our world. In your passion you demonstrated a hatred for evil and wrong, but a profound compassion and forgiveness for even the worst of sinners. As we discuss the people of the passion, fill us with empathy for both the victims and the perpetrators of evil. Through your presence within us and through the wisdom of your word, make us instruments of your healing and peace for those with whom we live.

3. Ask one or more of the following questions:
• Which of the people of the passion most intrigued you from this week's study?
• Which character from these accounts do you most want to imitate?

4. Discuss lessons 19 through 24. Choose one or more of the questions for reflection and discussion from each lesson to talk over as a group.

5. Ask the group members to name one thing they have most appreciated about the way the group has worked during this Bible study. Ask group members to discuss any changes they might suggest in the way the group works in future studies.

6. Invite group members to complete lessons 25 through 30 on their own during the six days before the next meeting. They should write out their own answers to the questions as preparation for next week's session.

7. Challenge the group to listen carefully and recognize the people of the passion during the liturgical reading of the Passion on Palm Sunday and Good Friday.

8. Conclude by praying aloud together the prayer at the end of one of the lessons discussed. You may want to end the prayer by asking members to voice prayers of thanksgiving.

Jesus said to his mother, "Woman, here is your son." John 19:26

The Mother of Jesus Stands at the Cross

JOHN 19:25–27 ²⁵*Meanwhile, standing near the cross of Jesus were his mother, and his mother's sister, Mary the wife of Clopas, and Mary Magdalene.* ²⁶*When Jesus saw his mother and the disciple whom he loved standing beside her, he said to his mother, "Woman, here is your son."* ²⁷*Then he said to the disciple, "Here is your mother." And from that hour the disciple took her into his own home.*

JOHN 2:1–5 ¹*On the third day there was a wedding in Cana of Galilee, and the mother of Jesus was there.* ²*Jesus and his disciples had also been invited to the wedding.* ³*When the wine gave out, the mother of Jesus said to him, "They have no wine."* ⁴*And Jesus said to her, "Woman, what concern is that to you and to me? My hour has not yet come."* ⁵*His mother said to the servants, "Do whatever he tells you."*

The gospel of John tells us that Jesus joined his mother and his beloved disciple as mother and son immediately before his death. Within the space of three verses (19:25–27) the word "mother" appears no less than five times. The mother of Jesus becomes the mother of the disciple. The words "mother" and "hour" tie the death of Jesus to his first great sign in the gospel (2:1–5). The "hour" of Jesus is the cross (12:23; 13:1; 17:1). At the wedding feast, Jesus' "hour has not yet come" (2:4); at the death of Jesus, "from that hour" or "because of that hour" (19:27), the beloved disciple took the mother "into his own home."

The gospel of John presents the mother of Jesus quite differently than the other gospels. In Luke and Matthew, Mary plays a prominent role in the birth and infancy accounts of Jesus. In John, the mother of Jesus is presented as the ideal believer both at the beginning of Jesus' ministry and at the cross. "Do whatever he tells you" (2:5), Mary said, as she initiated the first great sign of Jesus. At the cross, Mary stood near the cross of Jesus along with other women from Galilee and the beloved disciple. Mary's presence at the beginning and the end expresses her enduring faithfulness. Faith in its early stages may depend on signs and wonders; but in the end, faith involves perseverance, remaining with Jesus.

Though we have all known pain and grief, few of us know the incomparable suffering of a mother for her dying child. Mary's grief starkly reminds us that the crucifixion is rooted in the Incarnation—the human, physical, emotional reality of God's Word dying on the cross. On a human level, Jesus entrusted his mother to his disciple so that he would take care of her, and she would extend her maternal care for him. On a spiritual level, Jesus creates a new family, woman and disciple, mother and son, as he gave over his spirit. As Jesus dies, the church is born. Within that church, Mary is the ideal believer, mother of all disciples. She continues to tell her children everywhere, "Do whatever he tells you," and leads her children to ever deeper faith.

Reflection and discussion

• Mary said, "Do whatever he tells you." What is Jesus telling me to do?

• How is Mary presented differently in the various gospels?

• What aspect of Mary's faith do I most want to imitate?

• In what way can we say that the church is born as Jesus dies?

Prayer

Son of Mary, you cared for your mother and your beloved disciple while dying on the cross. Thank you for offering me the maternal care of your mother and help me to imitate her faith in you.

The centurion and those with him were terrified and said,
"Truly this man was God's Son!" Matt 27:54

The Centurion Professes Faith in Jesus

MATTHEW 27:45–54 ⁴⁵*From noon on, darkness came over the whole land until three in the afternoon.* ⁴⁶*And about three o'clock Jesus cried with a loud voice, "Eli, Eli, lema sabachthani?" that is, "My God, my God, why have you forsaken me?"* ⁴⁷*When some of the bystanders heard it, they said, "This man is calling for Elijah."* ⁴⁸*At once one of them ran and got a sponge, filled it with sour wine, put it on a stick, and gave it to him to drink.* ⁴⁹*But the others said, "Wait, let us see whether Elijah will come to save him."*

⁵⁰*Then Jesus cried again with a loud voice and breathed his last.* ⁵¹*At that moment the curtain of the temple was torn in two, from top to bottom. The earth shook, and the rocks were split.* ⁵²*The tombs also were opened, and many bodies of the saints who had fallen asleep were raised.* ⁵³*After his resurrection they came out of the tombs and entered the holy city and appeared to many.* ⁵⁴*Now when the centurion and those with him, who were keeping watch over Jesus, saw the earthquake and what took place, they were terrified and said, "Truly this man was God's Son!"*

I n the Roman armies the centurion was the commander of a company of soldiers and the backbone of the army. Earlier in the gospel Jesus had praised the faith of a centurion who described himself as "a man under authority, with soldiers under me" (Matt 8:5–13). There is no indication that the centurion at the cross was the same person, but centurions are always presented with positive qualities in the gospels and in Acts (see the accounts of Cornelius in Acts 10:1–8 and Julius in Acts 27:1–6).

Though the centurion at the cross is not named in the gospels, later tradition gave him the name Longinus and honored him as a Christian saint. Presumably this man was in charge of the crucifixion and its details: the walk to Golgotha, offering Jesus the bitter drink, the division of his clothing, and the nailing to the cross between two bandits. Then the centurion and his soldiers witness the last three hours of Jesus' life as they "kept watch over him" (verse 36, 54).

At the moment of Jesus' death, Matthew reports that the earth exploded with a series of awesome signs. The tearing of the temple veil, the earthquake, the splitting of rocks, and the opening of tombs were all the kinds of events that Jewish writings had used to describe the endtime. Matthew describes these events as expressing the significance of the death of Jesus. It was the end of the era of the earthly temple and the birth pangs of a new and final age of salvation.

Witnessing the death of Jesus and the overwhelming events which follow, the centurion and his soldiers are "terrified" (verse 54). The word expresses the trembling awe that frequently overwhelms those who witness divine signs in the Bible. It is the same awesome terror or sacred fear occasioned by the sight of Jesus walking on the sea (Matt 14:26). The awful crucifixion and death of Jesus becomes divine revelation for these Gentile soldiers. Matthew's passion account comes to a climax in their unified confession of Christian faith: "Truly this man was God's Son!"

Their confession of faith vindicates Jesus over against all the mockers who had employed the same title in derision while Jesus was dying (27:40). The centurion and his soldiers represent the vast multitudes from throughout the Roman empire who will come to faith in Jesus following his resurrection.

Reflection and discussion

• Why would Matthew spotlight the Roman centurion as the one who proclaims the truth that Jesus is the son of God?

• Who is under my authority? Am I a witness to Christ for those under my authority and those whom I can influence?

• What happened inside the centurion as he kept watch over Jesus during his final three hours? What happens inside me as I meditate on the crucifix or the cross of Jesus?

Prayer

Crucified Savior, you were tortured and killed by foreign troops, yet you gave them faith at the moment of your death. Increase my faith and forgive my sins as I look to your cross.

Many women were also there, looking on from a distance; they had followed Jesus from Galilee. Matt 27:55

The Women of Galilee Remain with Jesus

LUKE 8:1–3 *¹Soon afterwards he went on through cities and villages, proclaiming and bringing the good news of the kingdom of God. The twelve were with him, ²as well as some women who had been cured of evil spirits and infirmities: Mary, called Magdalene, from whom seven demons had gone out, ³and Joanna, the wife of Herod's steward Chuza, and Susanna, and many others, who provided for them out of their resources.*

MARK 15:40–41 *⁴⁰There were also women looking on from a distance; among them were Mary Magdalene, and Mary the mother of James the younger and of Joses, and Salome. ⁴¹These used to follow him and provided for him when he was in Galilee; and there were many other women who had come up with him to Jerusalem.*

The many women who were "looking on from a distance" during the crucifixion and death of Jesus were followers of Jesus from his ministry in Galilee. These women are far enough away from the cross of Jesus so as not to give active assent to what was happening, but close enough to be sympathetic witnesses to these climactic events. Their presence during these dark hours of Jesus is a stark reminder of the flight of the chosen "twelve" and their glaring absence at the cross. Among these "many women," the gospels mention a few by name. Mary Magdalene is the first named in each listing of the Galilean female followers. In addition Mark names another Mary and Salome. Matthew adds "the mother of the sons of Zebedee" (Matt 27:56).

The terms used to describe these Galilean women are words that refer to faithful discipleship. They "followed Jesus" through his life in Galilee and his journey to Jerusalem; they "provided for him" (Luke 8:3; Mark 15:41), a term referring to their service of Jesus in ministering to the needs of his mission; and they "came up with him to Jerusalem" (Mark 15:41), words referring to their unity with him in the way of suffering and the fulfillment of his mission at the cross. Their faithful following and service is a model for all future disciples.

The gospel writers found it important to note that the women were there looking on. They must have been heartbroken and bewildered to see Jesus dead on the cross. The proclaimer of the good news of God's kingdom, the one in whom they had learned to put their trust, had been executed in the most humiliating way. But the women loved so much that they could not leave him. Love clings to Christ when the intellect cannot understand.

These women form a link between the Galilean ministry of Jesus and the pascal events of his passion, death, and resurrection. Mary Magdalene and the other Mary, the mother of James and Joseph, watched as Jesus was laid in the tomb and they sat facing the tomb in silent vigil. They, along with Salome, will be the first to discover the empty tomb and to encounter the Risen Christ (Mark 15:47–16:1). They are the consistent witnesses through the Galilean ministry, to the cross, to the tomb, and to the resurrection.

Reflection and discussion

• What are the most important qualities of discipleship? How do the women of Galilee demonstrate these qualities?

• How do the evangelists starkly contrast these women of Galilee with the twelve male disciples of Jesus?

• What do these women teach me about faithful discipleship?

• When my faith is tested, do I stand at the cross, look on from a distance, or run away?

Prayer

Jesus, I look upon your cross and realize that you have surrendered all in faithfulness to the truth you proclaimed throughout your life. Teach me how to be a faithful disciple so that I will follow you throughout my life, even to the cross.

Joseph of Arimathea went boldly to Pilate and asked for the body of Jesus. Mark 15:43

Joseph of Arimathea Lays the Body of Jesus in the Tomb

MARK 15:42–46 ⁴²*When evening had come, and since it was the day of Preparation, that is, the day before the sabbath,* ⁴³*Joseph of Arimathea, a respected member of the council, who was also himself waiting expectantly for the kingdom of God, went boldly to Pilate and asked for the body of Jesus.* ⁴⁴*Then Pilate wondered if he were already dead; and summoning the centurion, he asked him whether he had been dead for some time.* ⁴⁵*When he learned from the centurion that he was dead, he granted the body to Joseph.* ⁴⁶*Then Joseph bought a linen cloth, and taking down the body, wrapped it in the linen cloth, and laid it in a tomb that had been hewn out of the rock. He then rolled a stone against the door of the tomb.*

oseph of Arimathea was a respected member of the Jewish council in Jerusalem, the Sanhedrin, the very body that had handed Jesus over to the Romans to be executed. His relationship to Jesus during his lifetime is unclear in the gospels: Mark tells us that he was "waiting expectantly for the kingdom of God" (verse 43), meaning that he was open and responsive to the message of Jesus. Matthew and John call him a "disciple" of Jesus (Matt 27:57), but John notes that he is a "secret" disciple out of fear of the Jewish leaders (John 19:38). But somehow the passion of Jesus had stirred the heart of Joseph and removed his fears. His boldness is a strong contrast to the cowardly disciples who had fled from the passion. Joseph did what the disciples of Jesus should have done: he courageously associated himself with the crucified Jesus and gave him a proper burial.

The Romans often left the bodies at the site of crucifixion for the wild beasts and birds to scavenge. But according to Jewish practice, a body should not be left on the cross overnight (Deut 21:22–23), and the law forbade burial after the Sabbath had begun. Since Jesus died at about 3:00 PM on Friday, and the Sabbath began at sundown, there was little time. Joseph of Arimathea went to the procurator and petitioned for the body of Jesus. Three times the text emphasizes that Jesus was dead (verse 44–45) and then tells us that Pilate granted the body to Joseph.

It must have been a profoundly mysterious experience to take down the lifeless body of Jesus from the cross, tenderly wrap it in the linen cloth, and carry it to its rocky tomb. Joseph laid his body on the prepared slab within the tomb and rolled the heavy stone into its groove against the tomb's door (verse 46). Matthew adds that the tomb was "his own new tomb, which he had hewn in the rock" (Matt 27:60). Jews often carved their family tombs from limestone outside the walls of Jerusalem. After burying the body of Jesus, Joseph left that sacred tomb, resigned to the fact that the once vibrant body of Jesus had found its place of rest.

Reflection and discussion

• Am I a fearful, secret disciple or a bold, courageous one?

• What makes some people heroic and others cowardly in the face of crisis?

• Imagine taking the lifeless body of Jesus from the cross and placing it in a tomb. How does this feel?

Prayer

Executed Lord, you have made holy all graves and made them beds of hope for all who trust in you. When my body lies in dust, may I live with you forever.

Nicodemus, who had at first come to Jesus by night,
also came, bringing a mixture of myrrh and aloes. John 19:39

Nicodemus Prepares the Body of Jesus for Burial

JOHN19:38–42 ³⁸*After these things, Joseph of Arimathea, who was a disciple of Jesus, though a secret one because of his fear of the Jews, asked Pilate to let him take away the body of Jesus. Pilate gave him permission; so he came and removed his body.* ³⁹*Nicodemus, who had at first come to Jesus by night, also came, bringing a mixture of myrrh and aloes, weighing about a hundred pounds.* ⁴⁰*They took the body of Jesus and wrapped it with the spices in linen cloths, according to the burial custom of the Jews.* ⁴¹*Now there was a garden in the place where he was crucified, and in the garden there was a new tomb in which no one had ever been laid.* ⁴²*And so, because it was the Jewish day of Preparation, and the tomb was nearby, they laid Jesus there.*

JOHN 3:1–12 ¹*Now there was a Pharisee named Nicodemus, a leader of the Jews.* ²*He came to Jesus by night and said to him, "Rabbi, we know that you are a teacher who has come from God; for no one can do these signs that you do apart from the presence of God."* ³*Jesus answered him, "Very truly, I tell you, no one can see the kingdom of God without being born from above."* ⁴*Nicodemus said to him, "How can anyone be born after having grown old? Can one enter a second time* *into the mother's womb and be born?"* [5]*Jesus answered, "Very truly, I tell you, no one can enter the kingdom of God without being born of water and Spirit.* [6]*What is born of the flesh is flesh, and what is born of the Spirit is spirit.* [7]*Do not be astonished that I said to you, 'You must be born from above.'* [8]*The wind blows where it chooses, and you hear the sound of it, but you do not know where it comes from or where it goes. So it is with everyone who is born of the Spirit."* [9]*Nicodemus said to him, "How can these things be?"* [10]*Jesus answered him, "Are you a teacher of Israel, and yet you do not understand these things?* [11]*Very truly, I tell you, we speak of what we know and testify to what we have seen; yet you do not receive our testimony.* [12]*If I have told you about earthly things and you do not believe, how can you believe if I tell you about heavenly things?"*

We don't know much about Nicodemus; we see him only in the gospel of John and he is a mysterious figure throughout. We know that he was a Pharisee, a Jewish leader in Jerusalem, and a teacher of Israel. In the passion account he appears with Joseph of Arimathea, and together they represent disciples who had gradually come to faith in Jesus despite their fears and the darkness of doubts. Though Nicodemus had not professed faith in Jesus openly, nevertheless, he was with Jesus at the end and served him splendidly in death.

Nicodemus had first come to Jesus at night (3:2; 19:39), a darkness of confusion and fear. He acknowledged Jesus as a rabbi, a teacher from God, and a worker of wonders (3:2), and Jesus tried to build on this limited understanding. Jesus' metaphor of rebirth means that a person must be "born again" and "born from above" in order to live in God's kingdom, an experience through water and the Holy Spirit (3:3–7). This new life is not only a human response to God; it is the initiative of God within the person. Nicodemus is baffled and Jesus explains that the Spirit, like the wind, is beyond human control or rational understanding (3:8).

After the lifeless body of Jesus was taken away from the cross by Joseph, Nicodemus came with a huge amount of spices for the burial of Jesus (19:39). Together they reverently wrapped the body of Jesus with the myrrh and aloes in linen cloths and carried him to the garden where they buried him in the new tomb carved in the rocks (19:40–42). The sheer quantity of spices with which they prepared the body of Jesus was extraordinary. The extravagance recalls the "pound of costly perfume" (12:3) that Mary of Bethany poured on the feet of Jesus to prepare him, as he said, "for the day of my burial" (12:7). The lavishness of the burial expresses the royalty of Christ as well as the extravagant nature of Nicodemus' love for his Messiah.

Clearly the faith of Nicodemus grew from his first encounter with Jesus to his burial as God's Spirit who blows where it wills (3:8) worked within him. He had come out of the darkness of fear into the light of open identification with Jesus and those who mourned him.

Reflection and discussion

• Have I ever experienced the spiritual darkness and confusion of Nicodemus?

• What are the aspects of birth that Nicodemus and Jesus were thinking of?

• What does it mean to be "born again"? Where am I in the birthing process?

• Have I ever experienced the uncontrollable nature of God's Spirit, blowing "where it chooses" (verse 8)? Where is God's Spirit blowing me?

• What does the presence of Nicodemus at the burial of Jesus teach me about the birth and development of faith?

Prayer

Jesus, I come to you perplexed and searching, longing for new life. Send your Holy Spirit to work in my life, to bring me into the light, to deepen my faith, and draw me closer to you

**Early on the first day of the week, while it was still dark,
Mary Magdalene came to the tomb.** John 20:1

Mary Magdalene
Comes to the Tomb

JOHN 20:1–2, 11–18 *¹Early on the first day of the week, while it was still dark, Mary Magdalene came to the tomb and saw that the stone had been removed from the tomb. ²So she ran and went to Simon Peter and the other disciple, the one whom Jesus loved, and said to them, "They have taken the Lord out of the tomb, and we do not know where they have laid him."*

¹¹But Mary stood weeping outside the tomb. As she wept, she bent over to look into the tomb; ¹²and she saw two angels in white, sitting where the body of Jesus had been lying, one at the head and the other at the feet. ¹³They said to her, "Woman, why are you weeping?" She said to them, "They have taken away my Lord, and I do not know where they have laid him." ¹⁴When she had said this, she turned around and saw Jesus standing there, but she did not know that it was Jesus. ¹⁵Jesus said to her, "Woman, why are you weeping? Whom are you looking for?" Supposing him to be the gardener, she said to him, "Sir, if you have carried him away, tell me where you have laid him, and I will take him away." ¹⁶Jesus said to her, "Mary!" She turned and said to him in Hebrew, "Rabbouni!" (which means Teacher). ¹⁷Jesus said to her, "Do not hold on to me, because I have not yet ascended to the Father. But go to my brothers and say to them, 'I am ascending to my Father and your Father, to my God and your God.'" ¹⁸Mary Magdalene went and announced to the disciples, "I have seen the Lord"; and she told them that he had said these things to her.

The gospels consistently identify this Mary by her own town of origin (Magdala, on the western shore of the Sea of Galilee), not by reference to a husband or son. This identification probably means that she had neither husband nor son and that she controlled her own property. The four gospels are unanimous in placing Mary Magdalene at the cross of Jesus and as a witness to the resurrection. She is presented as the single, consistent witness to the ministry of Jesus in Galilee, and to his suffering, death, and resurrection in Jerusalem.

In the dark hours of the morning Mary Magdalene searched for Jesus at the tomb and discovered that the stone had been rolled away. The only possible explanation for the absence of his body in the pre-resurrection world was grave robbing: "They have taken the Lord out of the tomb" (verses 2, 13). The only possible response was tears of grief (verses 11, 13, 15).

Mary's transformation occurred as Jesus called her by name. She recognized Jesus when she heard him call out her name: "Mary!" (verse 16). Jesus, the Good Shepherd, had said that he calls his own sheep by name and they hear and know his voice (10:3–4). She responded to his voice: "Rabbouni," which means "my teacher/master." Yet Mary's relationship with Jesus could no longer be the same as during his physical life on earth. Jesus tells her that she can no longer "hold on" to him (verse 17), as if he were still in the flesh. Mary and all disciples had to adjust to a new way of knowing Jesus as he ascended to the Father. The passing of Jesus from this world to the Father creates a new situation in which the God and Father of Jesus is also the God and Father of all his disciples (verse 17).

Mary Magdalene passed from the paralysis of weeping in the darkness to the apostolic faith of a disciple. "I have seen the Lord" (verse 18), she proclaimed. With the new understanding of resurrection faith, Mary received the first missionary mandate and she proclaimed the good news of the risen Lord.

Reflection and discussion

• What is the unique role of Mary Magdalene in all four of the gospels?

• Have I ever had a transforming experience in any way similar to that of Mary Magdalene?

• How are the people of the passion transformed from the darkness of the passion to the light of Easter faith?

Prayer

Risen Lord, you showed yourself to your disciples and transformed their weeping into joy. Enliven my faith and turn my darkness to light, my despair to hope, my disbelief to the fullness of confident trust.

SUGGESTIONS FOR FACILITATORS, GROUP SESSION 6

1. Welcome group members and make any final announcements.

2. You may want to pray this prayer as a group:

Lord Jesus, your gospels are filled with the lives of disciples who were drawn to you because of the wisdom, hope, healing, and love you offered. Mary of Nazareth, Mary Magdalene, Joseph of Arimathea, Nicodemus, the Roman centurion, and others came to entrust their lives to you through the experience of your passion. We gather together as people of the passion, as a community of your disciples. Transform our lives so that we may imitate and follow you through the way of the cross into the eternal life you promise.

3. Ask one or more of the following questions:
   - Do the people of the passion seem more like characters from the distant past, fellow disciples, role models to imitate, or heavenly saints?
   - In what way has this study challenged you the most?

4. Discuss lessons 25 through 30. Choose one or more of the questions for reflection and discussion from each lesson to discuss as a group.

5. Ask the group if they would like to study another book in the Threshold Bible Study series. Discuss the topic and dates, and make a decision among those interested. Ask the group members to suggest people they would like to invite to participate in the next study series.

6. Ask the group to discuss the insights that stand out most from this study over the past six weeks and how Holy Week and Easter will be different for them this year.

7. Conclude by praying aloud the following prayer or another of your own choosing:

Holy Spirit of the crucified and risen Christ, you inspired the writers of the passion accounts and you have guided our study during these weeks. Continue to deepen our love for the word of God in the holy Scriptures and draw us more deeply into the heart of Jesus. Gather us with the people of the passion around the cross of Christ, so that together we may claim the victory, the redemption, and the new life that he pours out upon us. Bless us with the fire of your love.